TENNIS DOUBLES

WINNING STRATEGIES FOR ALL LEVELS

BY
GREG LAPPIN
WITH KAY PFOUTS

PUBLISHED
KG BOOKS CO

Copyright © by KG Books Company

Printed in the United States of America by
Bolger Publications/Creative Printing
Minneapolis, Minnesota
First Printing, 1985

Published by
KG Books Company
5912 Schaefer Road
Edina, Minnesota 55436

You may order copies from the publisher. Try your
bookstore or pro shop first. Cover price plus $1.00 postage
and handling. Quantity/team discounts available.

ISBN 0-930425-00-6

Library of Congress Catalog Card Number 84-081014

Illustrations by Roger Boehm

Photos by Lori McQuarrie

Acknowledgements

Thank you to everyone who helped make this book possible.

To my parents — who started me in tennis.

To Jack Roach and Joe Walsh — who gave me my first chances.

To my colleagues — Tom Boice, John Mueller, and Kevin Ylinen.

To my wife, Dona — who gave me constant support during the writing of it.

To my students — who have been so great to work with for the last ten years.

And thanks to God for blessing me with such a wonderful life.

Contents

Introduction

I have written this book because I believe it fulfills an important need.

A thorough explanation of doubles court positioning and strategy is given at the level of the non-professional player. Serious students of the game and recreational players alike will benefit by reading it.

There are several reasons why this book will be helpful:

It is easy to understand.

I assume the reader has a basic proficiency. Beyond that nothing is assumed. All aspects of doubles are clearly explained. Catchy phrases and jingles are used in a fun way for easy memorization.

It is task specific.

Each chapter is devoted to a specific idea or task. Task relevant drills are listed to practice. Concrete tips are presented to insure improvement.

It is relevant.

Any level player can benefit.

It has a unique format.

Learning will take place by reading the manuscript and studying the diagrams. The On the Court sections list specific drills to practice on the court. Work on these! Initial performance has nothing to do with final performance. No matter what level player you are, practice these drills and you will master each section. Always be positive. The

Positive Self-Talk section is a check list. When you can speak affirmatively to each chapter, read on.

It is set up in a progressive fashion.
Chapters 1 and 2 are the foundation for the book. THESE ARE SECRETS THE PROS TAKE FOR GRANTED! Master these two chapters, and you are on the road to being a successful doubles player.

Chapter 3 lists the beginning positions. Doubles is a game where the same patterns develop over and over again. Generalizations or laws can be applied for situations that occur repeatedly. Chapters 4-6 give general laws to follow. Chapters 7-9 give general laws to follow when you are standing on specific spots on the court.

Different aspects of doubles are given individual attention in the rest of the book.

The "Let's Play" chapter brings everything together. When you have reached the end of the book, you will understand court positioning and strategy.

Attention is paid to the mental aspects of tennis, and answers are given to some commonly asked questions at the end.

I believe you are a successful player if you are improving and having fun. I know this book will add to your success.

The rhythm method
of ball control

Most tennis players understand the mechanics of an individual stroke. They know the correct grips to be used and
the right path to be followed with the swing. And good
mechanics are essential for good ball control. But once the
mechanical aspects of the stroke are automatic, continued
improvement depends on a sense of rhythm or timing. By
the time you have reached the level of an intermediate
player, your strokes are grooved. If you feel that improper
stroke mechanics will limit your development, then take a
few months off from competition and correct them. If you
do not have that kind of commitment or time, then do not
needlessly dwell upon minor flaws. Concentrate on
improving your sense of rhythm.

 The ball approaches a player with a number of variables
such as speed, spin, and height over the net. A player must
be able to synchronize the movements of her body and her
racquet to the variables in the movement of the ball.*
Developing an understanding of how the moving ball,
moving body, and moving racquet are all supposed to work

---

* This book is aimed at doubles players of both sexes and all ages. To avoid
awkwardness and confusion, the book alternates between masculine and feminine
pronouns.

PHOTO 1

together smoothly is fundamental for developing a solid doubles game. The development of this understanding is the development of a sense of rhythm or timing.

Just as music can be separated into notes, the rhythm or flow of a point can be broken down into parts: contact point, the ball traveling away from you, your opponent's contact point, and the ball traveling toward you.

1. **Contact point.** The goal of a player is to have both feet planted on the court during the entire swing. It is important to be aware if your feet are moving (Photo 1) or set (Photo 2) during your swing. And it is important to understand whether your feet are moving because of a lack of discipline or because of an excellent shot by your opponent that forces you to hit a ball on the run.

2. **The ball traveling away from you.** As the ball is traveling toward your opponent, you should be traveling toward a desired spot on the court. (Desired spots will be explained later.) This is one of the most important ideas in the book. How much court you cover — how many balls you can

PHOTO 2

get to — determines greatly what level of player you will be. The top players "move without the ball." This means they do a great deal of their movement — court coverage — while the ball is traveling toward their opponent. They do not have to do all of the work when the ball returns from their opponent. Most intermediate players hit and stand. They must do most of their movement after the ball is hit by their opponent. YOU CAN BE A BETTER PLAYER INSTANTANEOUSLY BY HITTING AND MOVING INSTEAD OF HITTING AND ADMIRING.

3. **Your opponent's contact point.** Here is where most players break down. There are two clues one may use to know when to stop moving toward a desired spot on the court and to get ready for your opponent's shot. When the ball bounces in front of your opponent, you should bounce into the ready position. If you are a more advanced player or your opponent takes a ball in the air, you should set when she begins her forward swing. (See Photo 3.) Stopping before your opponent makes contact

PHOTO 3

will allow you to be in a neutral, stable position when she does hit the ball. You can then move in any direction with ease and quickness. Failure to set up before your opponent hits the ball will make you set up late for your next shot. (See Photo 4.) THIS CANNOT BE OVERSTATED! This is a major cause of unforced errors.

4. **The ball traveling toward you.** You wish to move to the ball the split second you can recognize where it is going. You have to cover only one half of the court in doubles. This should make it possible to be stable for almost every shot. You will know that you have read the variables correctly if you are stable during your swing. (Again, this may not be possible if your opponent hits a terrific shot.)

These are the four components that make up the Rhythm Method of Ball Control.

1. Try to be stable when you make contact with the ball.

PHOTO 4

2. As the ball leaves your racquet, move toward your
    desired tactical position.
3. As your opponent starts her swing, pull up into your
    ready position.
4. When she makes contact with the ball, you are neutral.
    You can move quickly to the shot and be stable during
    your contact.

   If a person is sensitive to these components, then one
should be able to grasp the "Self-Evident Truths" discussed
in the next chapter.

On the court

1. Are you a stable person? Hit your shot and hold your
    finish without moving until the ball bounces on the other
    side of the net (practice routine only). Practice serving
    and volleying, and hold your finish on your volley until
    the ball bounces on the other side of the net.
2. Say "move" to yourself after the ball has left your

racquet to remind yourself to move to your desired spot.

3. Say "bounce" when you see the ball bounce on the other side of the net and feel your feet bounce into the ready position.

4. Repeat Number 3, saying "swing" when you see your opponent's racquet start to move into her forward swing.

5. Play out points. Hit the serve and jump into the ready position by the time the receiver has made contact with the return. Hit the return with stability. Move after the return. Get set when your opponent is about to make contact with your service return. Continue the proper movement throughout the entire point.

Positive self-talk

1. I am aware when I am stable or moving during all of my strokes.

2. I remember to hit and move after my shots. I do not hit and observe.

3. I am trained to assume a ready position just prior to my opponents' contact with the ball.

4. I have adequate time to get to most of my opponents' shots.

Self-evident truths

I hold these truths to be self-evident.

1. Persons can only learn through the use of the senses — sight, smell, taste, touch, and hearing.
2. Most tennis players do not use their senses.

Bill Tym, past president of the United States Professional Tennis Association, has stated, "There is no such thing as a good or bad player, just those who are well trained or poorly trained." I believe this is true. Perfect strokes are of little value if there is no perception of reality! Many players really do not understand what is happening on the court; they are not trained to use their senses.

We won't emphasize the senses of taste or smell. You will not have to examine the ball orally after each point; and, most players don't care much for the smell of their opponents after the first set. But this book *will* train you to see the signs obvious to professional players and to use the senses professional players use. Work at learning to "feel" your contact point, court position, and body position. If you can accomplish this, then you will have a solid and necessary foundation on which to expand your understanding of the game of doubles.

PHOTO 5

PHOTO 6

You need to be sensitive to three concepts: 1. Contact Point, 2. Body Position, and 3. Court Position

Contact Point

WHERE YOU MAKE CONTACT WITH THE BALL IS THE MOST IMPORTANT CONCEPT FOR A TENNIS PLAYER TO UNDERSTAND. Your contact point determines what shots are possible or "impossible" to hit. There is an ideal or optimal contact point for each stroke. On the ground strokes, you ideally would like to make contact about waist-high, out in front — roughly even with your front foot on a forehand and a shoulder width in front on a backhand — and a comfortable distance away from the body (Photos 5 and 6). You wish to make contact with the ball at eye level and more in front of your body on your volley (Photo 7). Making contact at these spots will enable you to put forth the minimum amount of effort to achieve the maximum amount of power and control. Making contact at less than the ideal spot — behind you (Photo 8), too high, too low, too close (Photo 9), too far away (Photo 10) — does not mean you have to miss the shot. But if the contact point is less than ideal, you must choose a less difficult target or hit with less pace or both. Specific situations will be described in the rest of the book.

Body position

You need to be sensitive to what your body is doing at the contact point. Are you stable or on the run? Is your body under control when you are stable and when you are moving? Is your weight shifting into your shot or are you pulling away from your shot? Is your body tense or relaxed? YOUR ABILITY TO CONTROL THE BALL IS DIRECTLY RELATED TO YOUR ABILITY TO CONTROL YOUR BODY! The goal is to be stable — have both feet firmly planted on the ground — during the entire swing. If you have to be moving while stroking, be aware of this and choose an easier shot.

Body position also is a function of contact point. An ideal contact point will allow for perfect body position and

PHOTO 7

body control. Notice the excellent body position in Photos 2, 3, 5, 6, and 7. Body adjustments will have to be made during the stroke if the contact point is awkward. Notice the poor balance in Photos 1, 8, 9 and 10. Obviously, if sudden, unplanned adjustments are required during a stroke, more errors will occur. Good footwork — striving to get in good position for every shot — is important.

Court position

You also need to know where you are standing on the court when you are hitting the ball. A sixth sense — an intuitive feeling of where you are on the court — is required at all times, because it is a factor in shot selection. The degree of difficulty in placing a ball to a specific target depends upon court positioning. For example, the farther you are from the net, the more difficult it will be to hit a winner. Several specific examples will be examined in the following pages.

THE POINT SHOULD BE CLEAR. Intelligent shot selec-

PHOTO 8

PHOTO 9

PHOTO 10

tion depends on an understanding of contact point, court position, and body position. There are only two kinds of shots: set-up shots and finishing (or put-away) shots. (Even with defensive shots you are still trying to set yourself up.) Set-up shots develop a point, while finishing shots end a point. A set-up shot could allow more time for better court positioning, force an opponent into a weak return, or force an opponent into a less desirable position on the court. But in every case, you expect your shot to be returned. You will be in a better court position with good balance and an easier contact point than your previous shot. This will allow you to control the point until you have a finishing shot, which is a ball that is so well placed or firmly hit that it cannot be returned.

OBEY THIS LAW! Hit finishing shots only when all three factors — court position, body position, and contact point — are in your favor. A great number of unnecessary errors are made attempting a finishing shot when a set-up shot should have been hit.

So far we have been very self-absorbed — focusing on these three factors only in terms of ourselves. But it is critical also to be able to recognize the contact point, body position, and court position of an opponent. Can you see the lack of sure footing in Photograph 1, the cramped contact point in Photograph 9, the poor weight transfer in Photograph 8, and the awkward contact point in Photograph 10? Can you see the good balance and contact point in Photographs 2, 5, 6, and 7? Very perceptive players even compute the three variables before their opponents make contact with the ball and logically deduce what kind of shot their opponent will hit next and where it will go. This process is called anticipation.

Does this ability to observe and understand these many variables in yourself and your opponents sound impossible to accomplish during a point? Not really. Remember you have already trained yourself to handle a multitude of variables in many other activities. Think how you anticipate when you are driving a car for example. A good driver is aware of oncoming traffic, the proximity of traffic behind the car, and the curves in the road ahead, all while maintaining a relatively constant driving speed. You have been trained to react in a certain way to the obvious variables.

Contact point, body position, and court position for you and your opponents are the obvious variables in tennis. The rest of this book will place these variables in specific situations. Read the material, study the diagrams, practice the routines, monitor your progress with the Positive Self-Talk sections, and let your senses make you a better doubles player! Good Luck!

On the court
1. Develop an awareness of contact point on ground strokes. When you make contact with the ball, say one of the following to yourself:
   Low — meaning you made contact below your knees.
   Good — meaning you made contact around your waist.

High — meaning you made contact above your chest.
Next try:
  Far — if you felt your arm was uncomfortably extended too far away from your body.
  Near — if you felt your arm cramped or feeling forced to pull back.
  Good — if you felt a comfortable angle between your arm and your body.
Then try:
  Front — when you make contact in front — defined earlier — of you.
  Behind — when you make contact behind you.

  Repeat the same for the volley with the exception of:
  High — arm stretched above you to excess where strength is lost.
  Good — making contact at eye level.
  Low — waist-high contact or lower.
  This can be repeated for all strokes.

2. Once a good perception of contact point has been established, monitor the type of shot you hit at each contact point. Learn to recognize your potential and limitations and choose a shot where you do not make an error.

3. Develop an understanding of your body position.
   a. Repeat Number 1 in the On the Court section of the Rhythm Method of Ball Control.
   b. Hold your finish on all strokes and feel if your weight is on your front foot or back foot.
   c. Notice what shots you are capable of hitting depending upon body position.

4. Develop an understanding of court position. Just after your swing is completed tell yourself where you are standing on the court. Say, "baseline," "service line," "no-man's land," "alley," "center," etc. You should notice your distance from the net and also your distance from the center of the court. Notice what shots you can execute from each area.

5. Repeat all of the above; say these things to yourself

when your opponents are making contact with the ball. Obviously focus on one idea per shot. (You may even start with seeing if your opponents are hitting forehands or backhands, and if they are left-handed or right-handed!)

Positive self-talk

1. I know where I make contact with the ball on my shots.
2. I know what shots I am capable of hitting depending upon my contact point.
3. I can see my opponents' contact point.
4. I am getting to where I can almost tell what my opponents can and cannot hit depending upon their contact point.
5. I am aware of my body position. I feel when I am stable or moving, when my weight is forward or on my back foot, and so forth.
6. I know what shots I am capable of hitting depending upon my body position.
7. I can see the body position of my opponents.
8. I can almost predict the success or failure of my opponents' shots because of their body position.
9. I know where I am on the court at all times.
10. I know what shots I am capable of hitting depending upon my court position.
11. I can see where my opponents are on the court.
12. I am beginning to recognize the potential and limitations in my opponents' shots due to their court position.

In the beginning:
the starting positions

All the players in a doubles match — server, receiver, server's partner, and receiver's partner — should be standing in the best tactical positions for the initial exchange. Each player is responsible for the one-half of the court on which she is standing. (See Diagram 1.) Here are the four positions:

Server

Stand in the middle of your half of the court. This places you in the best position to retrieve any service return. A player usually steps into no man's land — or no woman's land — because of the weight transfer of the service motion. This is fine. Just remember to jump back behind the baseline as the serve is traveling toward the service court. You should be two feet behind the baseline and set in the ready position by the time the receiver makes contact with your serve. Any return that is in will then have to land in front of you, not at your feet. You will not be caught pedaling backward for your shot. Of course, if you have a strong serve, or if your opponent cannot hit strong returns, you may wish to serve and immediately rush to the net. This technique, called serving and volleying, is discussed in the

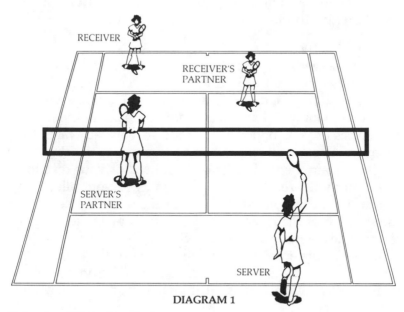

RECEIVER

RECEIVER'S
PARTNER

SERVER'S
PARTNER

SERVER

DIAGRAM 1

"Moving Violations" chapter.

Server's Job

Eliminate double faults. Place the serve with enough
speed or accuracy to force an average or weak service
return. Doing so will allow plenty of time for your next
shot. (Good depth is more important than speed.) Beginning
points with this advantage should result in your winning
most of them — if you get your first serve in. Remember,
the receiver may be able to take command of a point by
jumping on a second serve that lands shorter and travels
more slowly. Better to take a little speed off the first serve
and get a higher percentage in (60-80 percent). The server's
priorities are 1) consistency, 2) placement, and 3) power.

If you have a strong serve or are playing weaker
opponents, your serve may force the receiver into an error
or a weak return that your partner can poach — move over
and return a shot hit to your side of the court. For this
reason, it is a good idea to place the serve toward the center

T. This frees your partner from guarding her alley. She can then have more chances to pick off service returns that should return through the center of the court.

Server's Partner

As the server's partner, stand six to ten feet from the net on the other one-half of your side of the court. Exactly how close you should be depends upon the quickness of your reactions, your speed in chasing down lobs, and the tendencies of your opponents. Stand so you can watch the receiver. Also, stand within one to five feet of the singles sideline, again, depending upon the speed of your reactions. The faster you are, the more you can leave your alley open. It also depends upon the strength of the serve in relation to the strength of the receiver. If the serve is overwhelming the receiver, leave more alley open. She will not be able to place her return into such a small section of the court. If the serve sits up and the receiver smiles at you before she hits it, then forget about poaching. Just guard your own alley and half of the court.

Server's Partner's Job

Be as much of a threat and distraction to the receiver as possible while still protecting your own alley. Reading the three variables of court position, contact point, and body position in your opponent as she hits the return should tell you what to do. When the serve lands toward the singles sideline or is hit very softly, you must guard your alley. A serve down the center allows you to shift toward the center.

A variation in position is the Australian formation. If an opponent is consistently hitting crosscourt returns that your partner, the server, is having difficulty with, then consider what is called the Australian formation. (See Diagram 2.) In this formation the server's partner stands next to the center service line on the same side of the court as the server. This forces the receiver to return down the line. This change in tactics is designed to result in an error or a poorer return. If the server has a great forehand and a weak backhand, you may play regular positioning to the

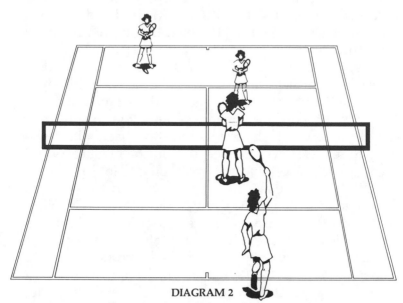

DIAGRAM 2

deuce court and Australian to the ad side of the court. This will protect the server's backhand. When using the Australian formation, the server should stand nearer the center service mark, because she will have to be running to the other half of the court after the service.

Receiver

Draw an imaginary line between the server and you. This line should bisect the service court. Or understand the two widest serves your opponent can hit. Bisect this. All serves are not created equal. This allows for equally good coverage of the entire service court. The speed and depth of the serve determine whether you stand in front of or behind the baseline. You want a minimum of footwork. Stand where you will need only one crossover step to meet the ball at the peak of the bounce. Most players hit their second serves slower and shorter in the service court than their first. Move in a step or two for the second serve.

AND MOVE AFTER YOUR SERVICE RETURN! Move

back behind the baseline after a weaker return, and move toward the net after a stronger return. Move in as fast and as far as you can. Use the Rhythm Method and stop when your opponents are hitting the ball. If you are caught deep in the back court, then it probably wasn't worth moving in.

As a receiver, your job is to get the return in and past the server's partner at the net. This is adequate. Ideally, you can place the ball effectively against the server and set up your partner. Effectively means placing your ball near the feet of the server. If she serves and stays back, aim higher (four to ten feet) over the net, so your ball will carry deeper. If she serves and volleys, then aim lower (one to three feet) over the net, so the ball will land at her feet near the service line. Judge the strength of the return. Move in behind a strong return and force the server into hitting a more difficult placement. Stay back after a weaker return. The great majority of returns will be hit crosscourt to the server (60-70 percent). Return down the line by the server's partner if she poaches frequently or if she leaves her alley unguarded 10-20 percent of the time. Keep her honest. You may lob off the return a great percentage of the time if the service is difficult to handle. Otherwise, lob 15-30 percent of the time to keep the serving team from anticipating your return. Lob more if it is effective. The receiver's priorities are to 1) get your return in play, 2) move the opponents out of position, and 3) add power (not at the expense of consistency).

Receiver's Partner

Stand with your heels on the service line, roughly three feet from the center service line. This is a transition position. A strong return allows you to attack forward. A weak return will have you standing still and defending. If the return is always strong, you may start in closer. Your jobs are many.

Protect yourself. The serving team has the advantage. The receiver is the first person who has the potential to hit a weak ball and set up the server's partner. If the server's

DIAGRAM 3

partner is well trained, she will be aiming the ball at you.
You, as a receiver's partner, are closer to her and therefore
have less time to react and return her shot. This is why you
start on the service line; this gives you adequate time to
protect yourself. If the server's partner is consistently
picking off the return and you are getting battered and
bruised, then move all the way back to the baseline. (See
Diagram 3.) This gives you more time to react.

Make calls on the serve. It is your job more than the
receiver's to call the serve in or out. If the serve is out, yell
"Out." If the serve is good, keep quiet. Silence tells your
opponents that the ball is good.

Read the movement of the server's partner. Face your
body at the server's partner; by doing this you can see her
movement to pick off the return earlier. You can also
observe her movement in relation to the serve. Does she
move properly? A lot of times a serve will be hit wide, and
the server's partner will move toward the center of the
court. The receiver is so busy hitting the return, she does

not notice this and hits her ball crosscourt. The server's partner is standing there and puts the ball away. The receiver blames herself for a poor return. In reality, the server's partner moved the wrong way only to have it work to her advantage. As a receiver's partner, you have to notice this and discuss it with your partner. Critique the server's partner's movement. Observe if she always moves with the ball. This alerts you to where she will be, and you will know what return to hit. If she moves incorrectly or too aggressively, you should be able to capitalize on it and place a winning return down her alley.

Do not move forward until you are certain the return will not be picked off by the server's partner. Many receivers' partners move forward when the serve lands, or when the receiver hits the ball. Moving at this time will leave the middle of the court wide open. You will also be moving closer to the server's partner and giving yourself less reaction time. This is not wise, unless you have easy access to a cheap dentist.

Stay on the service line and guard the middle of the court. If the server's partner picks off the return, you have the biggest part of the court covered. If an opponent hits a sharp angle for your alley, it will probably be a winner. You do not have enough time to cover all of your half. Once you realize the ball is not going to be taken by the server's partner, then turn your body and attention toward the server. Make the proper movements depending upon how the variables are affecting the server. If she has a really easy shot and looks as though she is aiming at you, then shuffle in and toward your alley. Give her a smaller target at which to hit in order to pass you. If the return is adequate, move toward the net and toward the center, since you are then guaranteed a higher contact point and are a threat to the server.

On the court
1. Play out points. Server, pause before you serve and make sure you and the other three players are in the

correct court positions.

Receiver. Hit your return with one crossover step and contact the ball at the peak of the bounce. Adjust in front or behind the baseline as you get used to the serve. After you have adjusted to the serve (one crossover step and contact), move in toward the net or back behind the baseline. Do not receive and stand.

Receiver's partner. Call the serve in or out. Do not move until the ball clears the net player. Critique how the return affects the server. Cover the appropriate court.

Server. Hit your serve and move back behind the baseline.

Server's partner. Try to anticipate where the return will go. If the serve goes wide, guard your alley. If the serve lands in the middle of the service court, stay still. If the serve lands in the center of the court, move to the center.

Positive self-talk

1. I hit my serve and move back behind the baseline.
2. I hit my return with stability because I need just one crossover step.
3. As a receiver's partner, I do not move in until I am certain the ball is past the net player.
4. As a receiver's partner, I defend the center if the return goes to the server's partner.
5. As a receiver's partner, I follow the return and cover the proper court when the server is hitting the ball.
6. As a server's partner, I know when to cover my alley and when it is possible to poach.

The most important line on the court: understanding shot selection

The "Self-Evident Truths" chapter pointed out that there are only two kinds of shots: set-up shots and finishing — put-away — shots. Remember finishing shots should be attempted only when all three variables — contact point, body position, and court position — are in your favor. This chapter will clarify the relationship between court position and shot selection.

A rule to follow is: Choose a set-up shot when behind The Most Important Line on the Court and realize that there is the potential for a finishing shot when you are in front of this line.

Where is this line? Imagine a line fourteen feet from the net parallel to the net. This line divides the service court into the front two-thirds and the back one-third. (See Diagram 4.)

When standing in front of this line, the front one-half or two-thirds of the service court, it should be possible — assuming good contact point and balance — to angle a shot for a winner or hit a shot by an opponent near you. Both of these shots are difficult to execute when standing in the back one-third of the service court or in the back court.

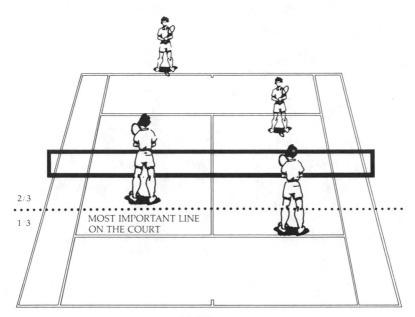

DIAGRAM 4

The reason it is much more difficult to angle the ball for a winner from behind The Most Important Line on the Court is that the margin of error is so small. If the ball travels the least bit wide, it is out; if it is not angled enough, it goes right to your opponent, who has an easy shot. (See Diagram 5.) All the pressure is on the hitter, and the risk is not worth the gain. Hit a set-up shot instead. Be content to place the ball near the feet and move in for better court position.

It is too difficult to blast a ball through an opponent from behind The Most Important Line on the Court because BALLS HIT HARD TRAVEL IN A STRAIGHT LINE. This means that a ball hit with a lot of speed will travel in a straight line for a fairly long distance. If both you and your opponent are on the service line, and you take a chest-high volley and blast it at her, it has to travel in a straight line and will hit her chest-high or racquet-high. This shot requires little racquet adjustment from your opponent and is not that difficult for a player of equal skill to return. (See

EASY FOR OPPONENT

VERY
DIFFICULT

OUT

DIAGRAM 5

Diagram 5.) A player is wiser to take that chest-high volley and return it at a slower speed to the feet of the opponent. The ball traveling at a slower speed allows the hitter time to move in front of the most important line. This is a great advantage. The ball placed at the feet also requires the opponent to hit the ball up to clear the net and — you hope — into your waiting racquet. (See Diagram 6.)

So, when you're standing at the service line and the contact point is below the top of the net, it is impossible to blast the ball. It will travel straight — straight into the net — or over the net beyond the baseline into the cheap seats. This ball must bend over the net and back down into the court. Balls can be made to bend by hitting softly or by using excessive spin. If you possess the ability to hit with spin, great! If not, then choose to continue developing the point with a set-up shot. Again, taking pace off the shot — hitting a softer shot — is more effective than hitting a powerful shot. This softer, well-placed shot will allow you to move into the finishing-shot zone for your next shot.

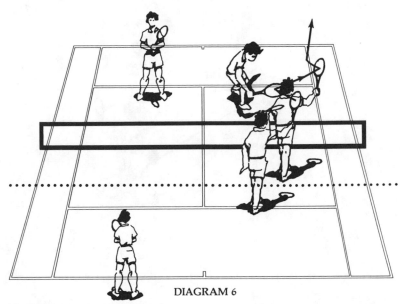

DIAGRAM 6

(See Diagrams 6 and 7.)

Standing near the baseline, you can hit the ball harder because it has a farther distance to travel. Your opponents are farther away though; this extra time allows them to return your best shots. The chance of blasting the ball directly at an opponent and creating an error is slim. Ground strokes are set-up shots — not finishing shots.

It is possible for a player to smash an overhead, place a volley, or drive a ground stroke for a winner from behind The Most Important Line on the Court. If a player possesses that talent — fine — the attempt should be made. Two concepts should always be kept in mind, however.

1. Commit very few errors — ideally none — from behind The Most Important Line on the Court. TRYING TO PUT THE BALL AWAY TOO EARLY IS PROBABLY THE GREATEST SIN IN DOUBLES! DO NOT GIVE THE MATCH TO YOUR OPPONENTS! Keep the ball in play from behind the most important line until a time for a finishing shot is present.

DIAGRAM 7

2. Never assume a winner has been hit from behind The Most Important Line on the Court. Players hit their shots, stand and admire them, and do not move to the next logical spot. (The book explains these spots later.) HIT AND COVER — DO NOT HIT AND STAND! ASSUME ALL BALLS WILL COME BACK. THIS ALSO TAKES THE PRESSURE OFF YOU. You do not need to hit winners from behind the most important line on the court.

On the court

1. The area in front of the most important line we'll call zone one, behind the line we'll call zone two. As you are stroking the ball, be conscious of which zone you are in.

2. Be aware of which zone you are in and tell yourself whether you will be trying for a placement — set-up shot — or a winner — finishing shot.

3. There is no pressure to hit a winner from behind The

Most Important Line on the Court. Play regular doubles points, working on consistency. One side serves until they make four unforced errors from behind the most important line. After the servers have made four unforced errors, then the receiving side serves.

4. Notice the court position of your opponents. Are they in zone one or zone two?

5. Notice what type of shots your opponents hit when they are in each zone. Do they choose set-up shots and finishing shots at the correct time? Can they execute these shots? Are they consistent or do they self-destruct? Do they have a favorite shot in each zone? Being able to answer these questions should help formulate a game plan against the opponents.

Positive self-talk

1. I know where I am on the court.
2. I know when to hit a set-up shot and when to go for a finishing shot.
3. I continually strive to decrease the number of unnecessary errors when standing behind The Most Important Line on the Court.
4. I know where my opponents are on the court.
5. I know whether my opponents are well-trained or poorly-trained players by the choice of shots they make when they are in a certain position on the court.

Champagne lunch:
understanding targets

Are your opponents good? Or do you make them look
good? Are you winning friends because you are so easy to
beat? Or are you winning matches? The answers to these
questions could have a lot to do with the targets you are
choosing on your shots. "Targets?!" "I am happy just to get
the ball in the court!" If you are a beginner, OK. If you are
an intermediate player, no! I believe you can hit the proper
targets on most occasions. The key is to know what your
potential and limitations are for each shot. This should
become more evident as you gain a greater understanding of
your body position, court position, and contact point and
as you come to realize that tennis is a game of the
appropriate or intelligent use of speed and height over the
net, as opposed to a game of power.

How do you know when you are hitting the proper
targets? OBSERVE THE CONTACT POINT OF YOUR
OPPONENTS! The game of doubles can be summed up in
one sentence: HIT THE BALL TO YOUR OPPONENTS'
FEET!

If you can make your opponents consistently have a
contact point below the top of the net, they will not be able

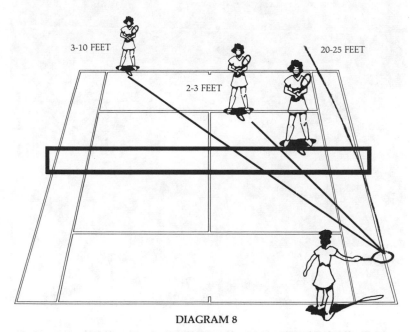

3-10 FEET

20-25 FEET

2-3 FEET

DIAGRAM 8

to place the ball exceptionally well or power the ball past
you. This should always allow you sufficient time to reach
any shot and to improve your court position, contact point,
and balance until you can put the ball away. The impor-
tance of striving to place the ball at the feet of the opponent
is the major factor in determining what speed, height over
the net, spin, and target on the court you choose.

If you exchange ground strokes from baseline to baseline
with an opponent, your target should be higher over the net
— three to ten feet — so the ball will carry deeper, nearer
the feet of your baseline opponent. (It is a myth to think the
better you get, the lower you hit in a ground stroke
exchange.) When you stay on the baseline and your
opponent moves to the service line, your shot must now be
hit two to three feet over the net and at a slower speed, so
the ball will drop sooner, therefore hitting your opponent at
her feet.

If an opponent stands very close to the net, then one
must lob over her head, because it would be impossible to

PHOTO 11

PHOTO 12

place the ball at her feet. (See Diagram 8.)

These examples should suffice. It is the choices you make on the use of speed, use of different heights over the net, type of spin, and target on the court that determine the contact point of your opponents on their next shot.

Most doubles players are "out to lunch." They give their opponents consistently high, easy contact points, and they are unaware how easy they are therefore making the match for their opponents.

Players who consistently give their opponents a contact point from mid-rib to mid-thigh will get "no lunch." This match will go on forever. Your shots never really hurt your opponents, and they can't help your cause, either.

Strive constantly to place the ball at the feet! I know this is a small target. Notice in Photographs 11-13 how the player has the same court position. Her opponents have hit her shots in all three contact point zones. Obviously, the contact point in Photograph 13 is the most difficult to return. But the more specific the command you give to your muscle memories, the more they will respond. If you find YOU DO NOT have the control to place your shot near the knees or feet of an opponent when they are in the mid court area, then SUNBURN THEIR EYEBALLS — LOB IT! Do not force it!

Doubles is a vertical game. You are placing the ball low to the feet or high over the head. You do not want to give your opponents chest-high volleys.

Doubles is also a logical game. It will be difficult to defeat opponents who have consistently good points of contact on their shots. A player must be aware of speed, height over the net, spin, and target on the court on each shot. Combining these variables determines the contact point of your opponents.

If you have the patience and discipline to try to place the ball at the feet of your opponents until the point goes your way, you will be celebrating many victories with a "Champagne Lunch!"

PHOTO 13

On the court

1. Stand opposite a partner a) baseline to baseline, b) baseline to service line, and c) service line to service line. Exchange shots back and forth. Aim your shots low at your opponent, trying to land your ball as near to your opponent's feet as possible.

2. All four people stand on the service line. Keep one ball in play. Volley shots as near to your opponent's feet as possible. Now, all four players stay on the service line. Players move in when they see they have placed a ball low to their opponents' feet and know a weak ball will come back.

3. Stand crosscourt baseline to baseline from a hitting partner. Drop and hit a ball. Have your opponent hit it back to you and follow her shot to the net. Keep aiming your shots near her feet. Notice as she gets closer and closer to the net that you must hit the ball lower over the net and softer to keep the ball near her feet. a) You

stay on the baseline the entire time. b) You move in
simultaneously against her.
4. Play out points. Say "high," "middle," or "low" corre-
   sponding to the contact point of your opponent. Notice
   if you are making the match easy or difficult for your
   opponent.
5. Use one ball with all four players starting at the baseline.
   Hit the ball back and forth, moving in when appropriate. The goal is to be aware of opponents' court
   position and place your shot near their feet. One point
   for the team that does this the best. First team to ten
   wins. Same drill but allow lobbing when it is too difficult
   to place your shots at their feet.

Positive self-talk

1. I can see the contact point of my opponent.
2. I know if my opponents have an easy or difficult contact
   point.
3. I understand that the contact point of my opponents is
   one of the major determining factors in the kind of shot
   they can hit back at me. I am responsible for the contact
   point of my opponents.
4. I can anticipate the shot of my opponents by understanding their contact point.
5. I understand that I have many choices on my shot such
   as speed, height over the net, spin, and target on the
   court. I decide what options to choose so I am able to
   place the ball at the feet of my opponents.
6. I know my limitations. When it is too difficult for me to
   place the ball at the feet of my opponents, I choose to
   lob.

Deep to deep:
close to close

An important phrase is deep to deep and close to close. This simple phrase tells you what to do in every situation. There is not one situation where this rule cannot be used.

Here is a definition of close and deep. When all three of our variables — court position, contact point, and body position — are in your favor, you have the potential to hit the ball harder or place it more accurately. When all three factors are in your favor you are close. You are able to aim the ball at the closer opponent. Place it by her or down at her feet. She will not have time to react to your shot, and you should have a winner or at least a poor shot back. This explains close to close.

Deep to deep applies when all the three variables are not in your favor. Two variables may be in your favor. You may have excellent balance and an acceptable contact point, but your court position may be poor. Unless all three variables are in your favor, you do not have a great potential for a put-away shot. You then should aim your shot at the opponent farther away from the net, or the deep person. Since she is deep in the court, she will have the least chance to put the ball away on you. This, also, will give

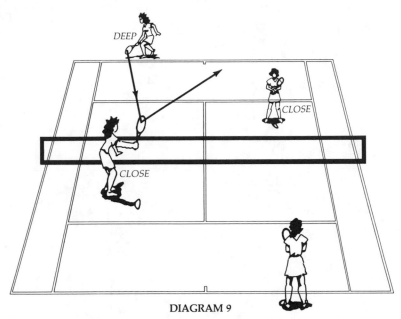

DIAGRAM 9

you the most time to recover for your next shot.

This may sound too simple to be significant, but consider what happens if this rule is not followed.

Deep to close. If you are deeper in the court and hit the ball to an opponent who is closer to the net — who will also probably have a better contact point — you stand a good chance of losing the point. Hitting deep to close makes it too easy for your opponent and does not buy enough time for you or your partner to react to her shot (Diagram 9).

Close to deep. Here, where all three variables are in your favor and you hit at the deeper person — the person farther away from you — you just give her extra time to react to your put-away attempt. She may be able to take that extra time and return your shot, which should have been a put-away. You let the fish off the hook (Diagram 10).

Here are some examples:

In Diagram 11, you are the baseline player. In position one you are behind the baseline, which is not great position for a baseliner. So, hit crosscourt to the other deep player.

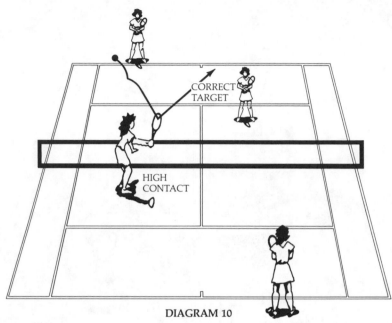

DIAGRAM 10

In position two, you are way inside the baseline. This is close because it is excellent court position for a baseline player. If you also have good balance and a good contact point, you should be able to pass an opposing net player. (Don't try, though, if she senses you're going there and closes off her alley.)

In Diagram 12 you are at the net. If you have a poor contact point, then be content to hit it back to the opposing baseliner or deep person. If all three factors are in your favor, then aim your volley toward the center T near the close person. The ball will pass by the feet of the net person and travel away from the deep person.

In Diagram 13 you are hitting an overhead. If you have a strong shot, go close to close. If you cannot hit a strong overhead, then go crosscourt to the deep person.

In Diagram 14, if you have an awkward position on your volley, then choose to go over the lowest part of the net to the person farther (deep) away. This gives you and your partner the most time to get ready for the return shot. You

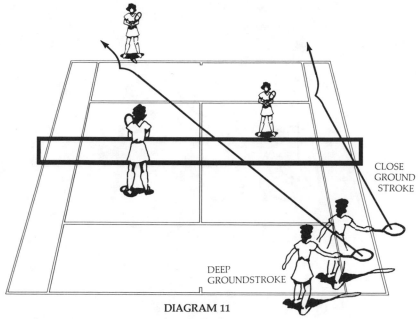

CLOSE
GROUND
STROKE

DEEP
GROUNDSTROKE

DIAGRAM 11

do not always have to aim right at the closer person. Here, go between them; why give them a chance to hit the ball?

Deep to deep and close to close is a good jingle to keep in your mind. If you go deep to deep, you should always have enough time to recover into good tactical position for your next shot. Since you are deep and do not have the potential for a put-away, going for their deeper person should also prohibit them from putting the ball away on you.

Hitting close to close should allow you to finish off the point with the first opportunity.

This concept should help your anticipation as well. (See the chapter on "Legalized Cheating.") If you can recognize when your opponents are the deep or close person, then you know what shots they will be choosing if they are a well-trained team. By your knowing whether you are the deep or close person on your side, you know to whom they should be aiming the ball.

If they do not follow the deep-to-deep, close-to-close rule with their shots, then you know they are either poorly

DIAGRAM 12

trained or cannot control their shots. In either case that should give you confidence.

On the court

1. All four players start on the baseline. Hit back and forth. One side stays on the baseline while the other side moves in. Baseliners, see which is the close and deep person. Hit to the deeper one until both get in front of The Most Important Line on the Court. Then lob them. When they charge in — if they both are even or equal distance from you — then go between them.

2. Place one up and one back on each side. Baseliners hit deep to deep crosscourt ground strokes to each other. Net players, if you pick off a shot, aim it close to close by the other net player for a winner. This assumes all the variables are in your favor. Baseliners, follow up to the net behind appropriate short balls.

3. All four players start on the service line. Hit volleys back

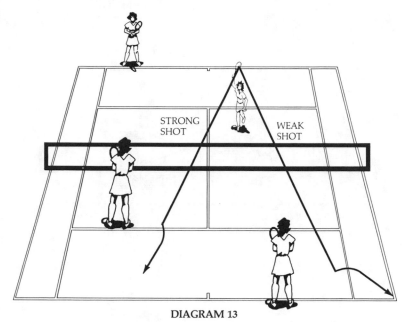

STRONG
SHOT

WEAK
SHOT

DIAGRAM 13

and forth. Go deep to deep and close to close depending
on the variables. If opponents are equidistant away from
you, aim low and between them.

4. Place two people at the net. The opposing team has one
at the baseline and one at the service line. Baseliners,
start the point with a lob. Net player, hit your overhead
near the service line opponent when the variables favor
you, and block it back to the baseline player when in
more trouble. Play out the point with everyone choosing
the correct targets.

5. Play out doubles points. Set up different playing situations and practice deep to deep and close to close.

Positive self-talk

1. I am aware of the three variables — contact point, court
position, and body position — from the "Self-Evident
Truths" chapter.

2. I understand from Number 1 whether I am a deep or

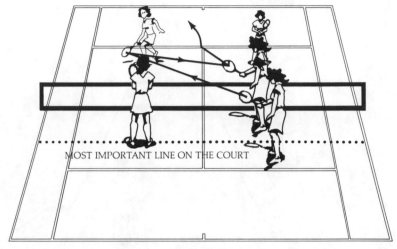

DIAGRAM 14

close player.
3. I can see if my opponents are deep or close during the point.
4. I always choose deep to deep and close to close targets.
5. Because I choose deep to deep I have adequate recovery time on my shots.
6. Because I choose close to close I put the ball away when I have the opportunity.

Boring is beautiful:
playing the baseline

The baseline is located far behind The Most Important Line
on the Court, and shots hit from the baseline should be
classified as set-up shots. Nevertheless, many players feel
pressure to hit a winner, or they show impatience and try to
end the point too quickly. Eliminate errors; do not self-
destruct; "Boring is Beautiful" is the rallying cry from the
baseline. Depending upon your level of expertise, your job
is to 1) get the ball in, 2) get it in and by the closer person
at the net, 3) get it by the closer person at the net and land
it near the feet of the deeper person, wherever she may be,
and 4) get it at the feet of the deeper person with spin or
speed. If things aren't in her favor, a good baseliner knows
to lob.

Your boredom will be successful or stressful depending
upon your ability to recognize our three variables — court
position, body position, and contact point. Here are the
various positions where your opponents can be on the
court:

**One opponent is at the baseline and the other is at the
net.** (See Diagram 15.) Your high-percentage shot is to hit a
safe ground stroke to the opposing baseline player (usually

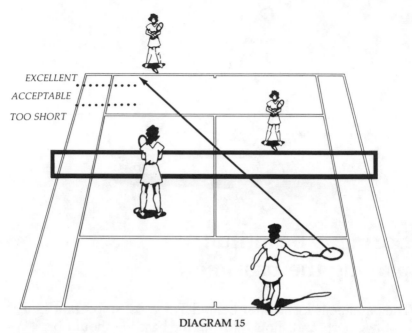

EXCELLENT

ACCEPTABLE

TOO SHORT

DIAGRAM 15

crosscourt). Aim the ball at least four to ten feet over the
net. This height should ensure good depth. Depth in itself is
a useful tactic. Your chances of blasting a winner are slim at
best. Your opponent is eighty feet away and has to cover
only one half of the court. If you cannot hit a shot that
hurts your opponent, then DO NOT HURT YOURSELF!

Overhitting a ground stroke at the opposing baseline
player can result in an unforced and unnecessary error.
Placing your ground stroke so it will land deep in the back
court will force your opponent to make contact with her
shot from behind her baseline. (See Diagram 15.)
Obviously, if you cannot hurt your opponent from the
baseline, then she cannot hurt you from behind her baseline
either. At worst, your shot will force an exchange of
neutrality. At best, it will force her into an error or poor
return from which you can then take charge of the point.

The opposing net player should not be a threat if your
shot is well placed. There is always an opening by her or
over her. An understanding of her court position in relation

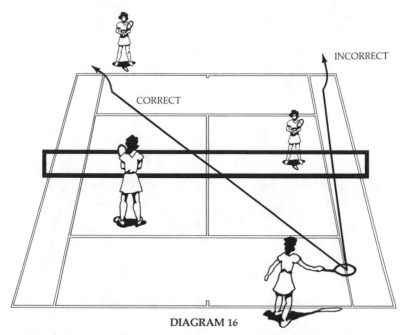

INCORRECT

CORRECT

DIAGRAM 16

to the three variables at your contact will tell you which opening to choose.

First, are you making contact near the doubles alley or the center of the court? It is obviously difficult to hit a shot down the line (into the alley) from the center of the court. If the net player is lined up even with you, the crosscourt is the open shot. (See Diagram 16.) If she is appreciably closer to the net strap than you are to the center service mark, then the line is open. (See Diagram 17.) THIS IS CRUCIAL TO UNDERSTAND! Many times a net person picks off a ground stroke hit crosscourt, and the baseliner thinks she has hit a poor shot or that the opposing net player is a great poacher. On most occasions, however, the net player is out of position, standing in the center of the court. The baseline player fails to recognize her opponent's position and hits her crosscourt ground stroke right into the waiting racquet of the net player. The correct shot in this situation is the alley left vacant by the net player.

When you are uncertain of the court position of your

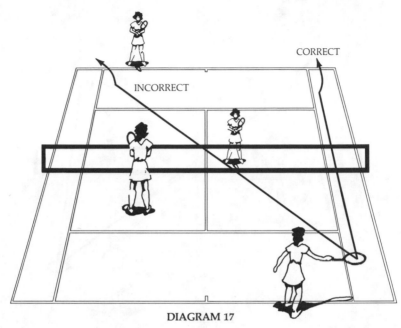

DIAGRAM 17

opponent, when you know you have poor body position or contact point, then LOB. DON'T FORCE THE GROUND STROKE BY THE NET PLAYER! TAKE THE EASY WAY OUT! If you can control the lob, lob over the person closer to the net. She will have the most running to do to get to the ball. In fact, you may wish to use this technique as an offensive tactic. (See the "Lethal Lob" chapter.)

One opponent is on the service line and the other is in the middle of the service court. (See Diagram 18.) Well-trained players understand that their opponents are not an equal distance from the net. This is tremendously important to recognize! The opponent closer to the net has excellent court position. It would be difficult to hit a ball by her or make the ball drop fast enough to land at her feet. Play her the same way as described in the previous paragraphs.

Your first choice then is to hit your shot toward the person standing on the service line. Use the appropriate speed and a low height over the net to land the ball at her feet. This will force her to hit the ball back softly, allowing

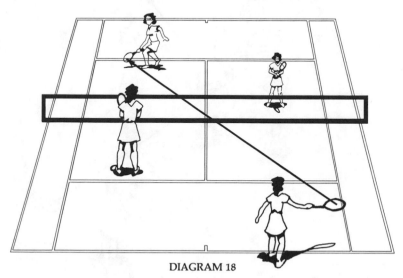

DIAGRAM 18

you plenty of time for your next shot. She cannot hit the ball hard; hard balls travel in a straight line. Her hard shot will travel straight into the net or straight over the net and out. Your low ball to her feet then will FORCE her to "bend" the ball back over the net to you. As mentioned earlier, balls bend by being hit one of two ways — by putting excessive spin on the ball, which the average players cannot do, or by slowing the shot down. Most players do not possess the softness of touch in the hands to accomplish this and will, therefore, miss balls hit at their feet.

If your opponent doesn't miss the shot altogether, she may pop the ball up softly so your partner at the net can put it away. This is the "Low and Go" play. As a baseliner, you place the ball LOW to the feet of the opponent on the service line. Your partner recognizes how your low shot handcuffs the opponent and moves toward the net as soon as possible to pick off the floating shot coming back. (See Diagram 19.) This is doubles teamwork at its finest! THE DEEP PERSON SETS UP THE CLOSE PERSON. The more

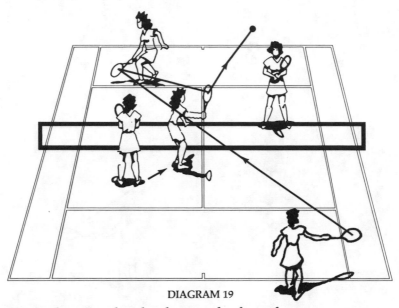

DIAGRAM 19

effectively your shot lands near the feet of your opponent, the more you move in from the baseline as well because you anticipate a weak return.

If you DO NOT have the control to place the ball low to the opponent on the service line, then your second choice is to lob the opponent who is closer to the net in the middle of the service court.

Both opponents are close to the net. If you are an exceptionally strong player, you may be able to place or power the ball by the opponents. As a generalization, your first choice is between them. (See Diagram 20.) This cuts down on the angle of their returns and is a larger target at which to aim, and your shot travels over the lowest part of the net. If you do not possess this high degree of ball control, then the first choice and easiest shot is the lob. Make your opponents scramble back and hit an overhead, which is difficult for most players. Remember, eliminate errors. Always take the easiest way out. Lob in this situation until you can gain control of the point.

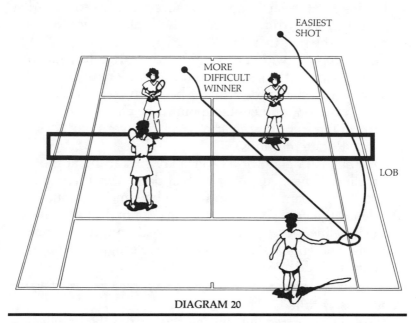

DIAGRAM 20

On the court

1. Practice hitting crosscourt ground strokes (working on contact point and balance) until you can keep the ball going several times over the net and with consistent depth. Keep ten balls going in a row that land behind the service line.

2. Stand on the baseline. Have your opponent stand on the service line. Practice hitting the ball landing at her feet. Keep your shot low over the net.

3. Drill with one player at the net and the other on the baseline. Opponents are lined up in similar positions. Practice:

    a. Baseliners, practice hitting shots away from the net person. As the ball leaves the opponent's racquet at the baseline and travels in front of the opposing net person toward you, notice if the alley is covered or open. Aim your shot into the open court.

    b. Exchange deep crosscourt ground strokes. Baseliner,

when you hit a ball short to the opposing baseliner, forcing her forward into the service area, try to place her return shot down to her feet. If both players get too close to the net, then lob.

4. Start the point with a serve and return. Receiver hits the return back to the server and follows the return to the service line. Server determines her own court position, body position, and contact point. She chooses to hit her shot to the feet of receiver or over receiver's partner's head. Rotate positions.

5. One ball is in play for all four players starting at the baseline. Players keep hitting ball deep. When a ball is short, that team rushes up for the ball and continues toward the net. The team that hits the ball short stays on the baseline, observing the court position of the opponents, and chooses the correct shot. Recognize if opponents are side by side or staggered.

Positive self-talk

1. I feel no pressure while hitting shots from the baseline. I know I do not have to hit winners.
2. When I am standing on the baseline, I always know where my opponents are on the court.
3. I know where my opponents are on the court and can choose the most effective shot.
4. I have the confidence and ability to hit my ground strokes deep to an opposing player on the baseline.
5. I recognize when an opponent is standing on the service line, and I have the ability to place the ball to her feet.
6. I can see my opponent at the net. I can place the ball away from her. She is no threat to me.
7. I know when I cannot get the ball by a net person. I choose to lob. There is no need to panic and lose the point.

The greatest sin:
playing the service line

Doubles is played ideally within ten feet of the net or at the
baseline. Few players are fast enough to hit their first shot at
the baseline and be next to the net for their second shot.
Therefore, many transition shots, shots hit while moving
from the baseline to the net, will be hit around the service
line.

As a tennis pro, I view committing unforced errors as the
greatest detriment to a player's game. I will be able to retire
a happy pro if I have convinced players their goal should be
the elimination of errors instead of the blasting of winners.

The service line is a tempting place to sin. Players believe
they are close enough to the net for the kill. In reality,
though, the service line is behind The Most Important Line
on the Court. The great majority of shots will fall into the
category of set-up shots and not finishing shots. A shot
from the service line may end the point because of a superb
placement or an error by an opponent. But one should
always treat a shot at the service line as a set-up shot.
Expect a return from your opponent and move into better
court position after your shot.

Let's examine our three variables of contact point, body

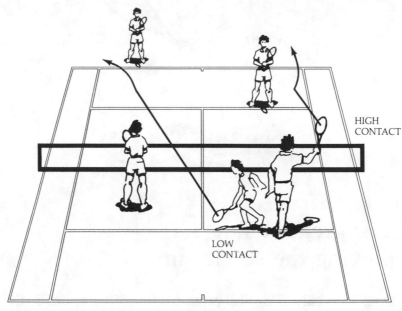

HIGH
CONTACT

LOW
CONTACT

DIAGRAM 21

position, and court position. The court position for you, obviously, is fixed at the service line. This leaves the court position of your opponent, your contact point, and your body position as the variables that determine shot selection.

Notice that your court position is identical to that of the opponent on the other service line in Diagram 21. If your contact point is good — above the height of the net — and your body is under control, then you would like to hit the ball to the feet of the opponent on the service line. He should make an error or hit the ball up to you. Move in while your shot is traveling toward your opponent, and you should be in position for an easy put-away on your next shot. If your contact point is low, then it would be difficult to put the ball through this player, so your shot is to the opponent on the baseline.

The court position of both of your opponents is identical to yours in Diagram 22. Your finishing shot should be placed equidistant between them. Do not give them a high ball or a ball directly at them. Placing a low ball through

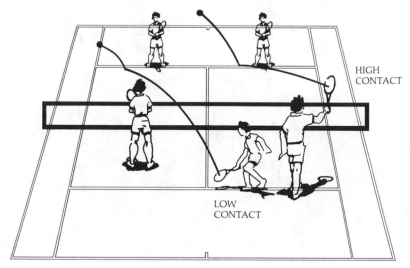

HIGH
CONTACT

LOW
CONTACT

DIAGRAM 22

the center should force a return back through your center.
THIS IS A BASIC LAW OF DOUBLES. BALLS THAT
TRAVEL THROUGH THE CENTER WILL RETURN
THROUGH THE CENTER. You and your partner can
converge on the middle. It will be difficult for them to fight
the flow and put a ball in the alley.

When you have a low contact point or awkward balance,
still place the ball to the same target, if possible, or along
the longest distance over the net. This will allow the ball to
pass over the lowest part of the net and allow the most time
for your recovery.

Your contact point has pulled you wide into the alley in
Diagram 23. When you are pulled wide — aim wide —
keep the ball in front of you. If your opponent does return
this ball, which you try to place at his feet, it again will
have to pop up to you or your partner, who has shifted
over. By choosing these targets, you are able to create the
situation where it is two against one. Remember to move in
front of The Most Important Line on the Court after your

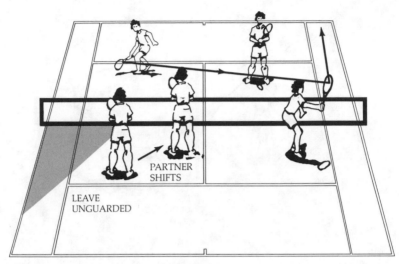

PARTNER
SHIFTS

LEAVE
UNGUARDED

DIAGRAM 23

shot to create better court position.

Notice one opponent has better court position in Diagram 24. It would be difficult to place a ball by him: you could only hurt this opponent by blasting a ball through him. This is risky. Your better choice is to hit a set-up shot at the feet of the partner farther from the net. Then move in, using your second shot as the finishing shot.

Both opponents are at the net in Diagram 25. If you have the presence of mind and skill, try a lob over their heads. If this is too difficult, then hit the ball as soft and as low as you can between them and hope for the best! A low ball will not give them a good contact point, and a soft ball will give them no pace with which to work. It should also give you more time to get in as close to the net as they are.

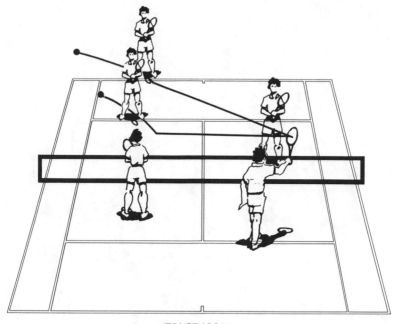

DIAGRAM 24

On the court
1. Drill with friends. Stand (and stay) on the service line. Have your opponents stand in various positions on the court as outlined in Diagrams 22-25. Understand your contact point and body position, and their court positions. Hit your shots to the correct target. Keep the ball in play as long as possible. Be aware if your ball is landing near the feet of your opponents. Rotate positions with your friends.
2. Do the same drills as Number 1. Now, move off the service line and play the point out as you would in a real game.

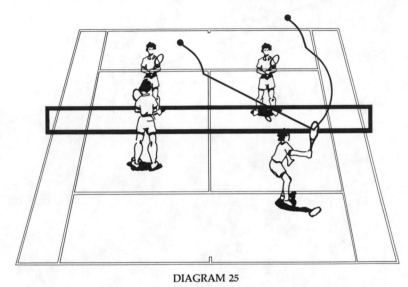

DIAGRAM 25

Positive self-talk
1. I know when I am on the service line during a match.
2. I know where my opponents are on the court.
3. I understand my contact point, my body position, and my opponents' court position, and I choose the correct target.
4. I am able to aim the ball by my opponents or at their feet.

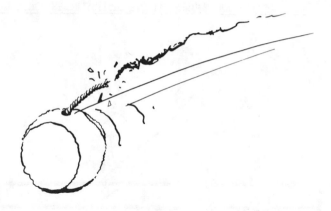

Never give a sucker an even break: playing the net

Ah! The net! The position for glory — a chance to put the ball away. If you play it right.

A lot of times, however, players at the net send easy balls back to their opponents, letting them off the hook. At other times, players will get excited at the opportunity for a winner, overhit the shot, and make an unnecessary error. NEVER GIVE A SUCKER AN EVEN BREAK! Your goal is to win points — not your opponent's gratitude.

Let us analyze playing the net in terms of our three variables. First, your court position. Effective volleyers play in the middle one-third of the service court — seven to fourteen feet from the net. When your opponents are hitting their shot, you want to be in the first one-third to one-half of the service court from the net. Being this close, no balls should be able to get low to your feet. You should get a minimum waist-high contact point. (See Diagram 26.) This distance is roughly a giant step and a reach from the net. (Reach the racquet out toward the net.) Your racquet should almost be able to touch the net (Photo 14).

Also, as a generalization, play "navel tennis." Keep your navel in front of the ball. This means your body should be

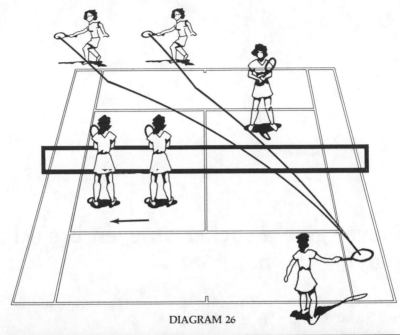

DIAGRAM 26

PHOTO 14

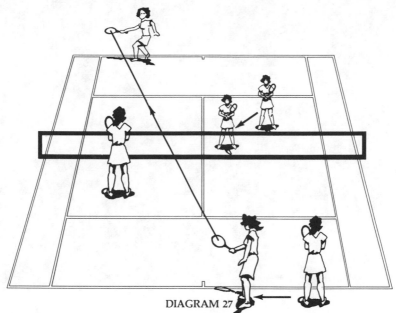

DIAGRAM 27

directly opposite — in front of — the ball when your
opponent is hitting her shot. (See Diagrams 26 and 27.) In
this way your opponent must angle the ball by you. If the
ball lands wide on the other side (Diagram 26), guard your
alley. Remember, keep your navel in front of the ball. You
are not all things to all people. Guard your alley and your
one-half of the court. Let them angle a shot crosscourt.

If a ball lands in the center of their court, be very
aggressive. (See Diagram 27.) Let them try to angle the ball
behind you. This is a difficult, low-percentage shot. Make
them prove they can hit that shot before you guard it.

The key is to be sensitive to your opponents' contact
point, body position, and court position and know how
much court you can give away (the area of the court they
cannot realistically hit a ball into), and which balls you can
pick off.

So keep these two concepts in mind.
1. Keep your navel in front of the ball when your opponent
   is making contact with the ball.

PHOTO 15

PHOTO 16

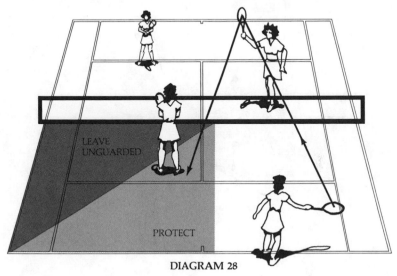

DIAGRAM 28

2. Be in the first one-third to one-half of the service court
   closest to the net when your opponent is making contact
   with the shot.

   What happens, though, when your partner behind you is
hitting the ball? YOU MAY LIKE HER, BUT YOU NEVER
TRUST HER! At the intermediate to advanced level of play,
you cannot be sure that your partner behind you will
always place the ball past the opposing net player. Therefore, shuffle back several feet diagonally toward the center
T. As the ball travels by you, step back with your inside
foot and have your navel face the opposing net player. (See
Photo 15.) Move back several feet only. (See Photo 16.)
This is far enough. It is unnecessary to move into the back
one-third of the service court — that's excess movement. By
now the ball has bounced for your partner to hit it. Your
opponent's body and racquet language will tell you if she is
going to hit it. When you see this, move back some more if
there is time. If not, get set and get down like a hockey
goalie and defend yourself. Guard the center of the court.

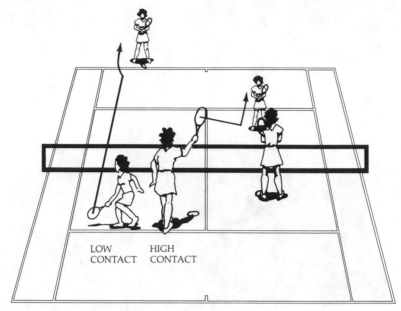

LOW   HIGH
CONTACT   CONTACT

DIAGRAM 29

Give away the sharp angle put-away (Diagram 28). When you see the ball will not be taken by the opposing net player, run two steps toward the net with your navel in front of the ball. Stop when the ball bounces. You are now in your original position and ready for the shot from the opposing baseline player.

Shuffling back and running forward is important for intermediate players. When you are back, you have more time to react to a shot from an opponent at the net. You have the center guarded when your opposing net player picks off the shot. And you can quickly get in to the net for good court position if the ball clears the opposing net player.

If you have mastered these concepts, you will always have the correct court position.

The court position of your opponent and your contact point and balance determine your shot selection. Remember the deep-to-deep and close-to-close rule. Here are some examples:

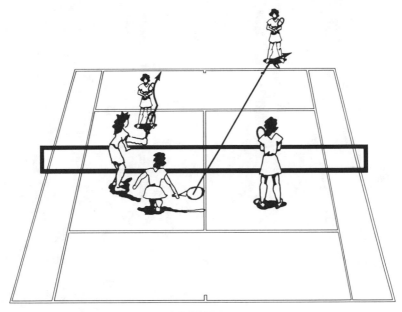

DIAGRAM 30

Here your opponents are one up and one back (Diagram 29). You are close to the net. If you have a good contact point and good balance, then aim at the center T. This will cross the feet of the net player and will angle away from the baseline player. Neither one should be able to return your shot. It is a winner due to placement — not power.

If you are not under control, then aim back to the baseline player and hope for an easier shot on your next hit.

In Diagram 30, your opponents have shifted on their side of the court. When the variables are in your favor, aim the ball straight ahead at the net player directly in front of you. Do not be concerned about hitting such close opponents. Control the ball to their feet, so they do not have time to react. Bruises below their kneecaps will heal in a few years. If you feel you cannot control the ball at their feet, then aim crosscourt to the baseline player.

In Diagram 31, both players are a great distance away from you. It would be difficult to blast a ball hard enough through them to finish the point. Your first choice is to

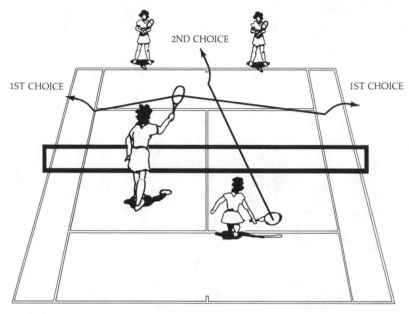

DIAGRAM 31

angle the ball off the court. If it is too difficult to angle the ball, then aim it deep through the center of the court. This will make it difficult for the opponents to angle a passing shot by you. Their options should be limited to a passing shot back through the center or a lob.

When both opponents are opposing you at the net, aim your put-away shot between your opponents and at their feet (Diagram 32). Do not give them the luxury of a ball at them or high. If a low placement between them is not possible, then place the ball as softly as you can to their feet. This will limit the speed of their return.

These examples should give enough insight into shot selection when playing the net. The deep-to-deep and close-to-close rule must be obeyed.

On the court

1. Practice volleying. Stand one-third to one-half distance from the net. Have a hitting partner stand on the

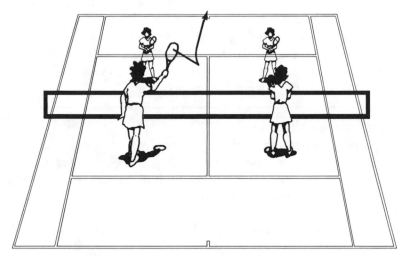

DIAGRAM 32

opposing baseline directly in front of you feeding you
balls. Aim easy shots at the center T. Aim difficult shots
back to the feeder.
2. Place four players in the traditional one up and one back
   doubles position. Net players, do not try to poach on
   balls but work on the movement of running up and
   shuffling back.
3. Do the same drill. Net players, concentrate on keeping
   your navel in front of the ball. Baseline players, keep the
   ball deep and away from the opposing net players.
4. Do the same drill. Net players, now concentrate on
   gaining sensitivity to guarding the alley or poaching.
   Poach a shot whenever possible. Baseliners, now feel free
   to burn the net player down her alley if possible. Play
   out the points.
5. Two players stand at the net. Two opponents stand at
   the baseline. Net players, angle volleys when possible.
   Hit volleys deep to the baseline when not. Net players,
   shift together as a team, playing navel tennis. Baseliners,

try to hit all passing shots, keeping the ball as low as possible.

6. All four players stand one step in front of the service line. All players try to hit balls low at opponents and through the center.

7. Play out points starting with a serve. Do not be concerned with the score. Critique the points, understanding as a net player if you chose the correct shots and were in the correct court position.

Positive self-talk

1. I am close enough to the net when my opponents are hitting, so I have the potential to put the ball away.

2. I know to shuffle back when the ball has traveled behind me and my partner is hitting.

3. I keep my navel in front of the ball.

4. I am sensitive when I should guard my alley and when I can poach.

5. When all four players are at the net, I aim the ball at the feet of my opponents. I do not try to overpower them.

6. I understand shot selection as a net player. I understand what close to close and deep to deep means.

The perfect player: go with the flow

What is your definition of a perfect player?

Someone who has perfect strokes? Maybe so, but they are of little advantage if the player cannot keep the ball in the court or understand proper shot selection.

Someone who can hit two lines with every shot — in other words, consistently hit winners? This is not possible. (Remember the chapter "The Most Important Line on the Court.") How many baseball batters hit a home run every time they are at bat? How many football teams score a touchdown on every play? None! It is just as improbable to hit all winners in tennis.

Someone who is so confident he doesn't have to play "First one in" on his serve. That is approaching greatness!

I know! Perfect Players blast the ball as hard as they can. Perfection is Power! Ugh! This is the greatest misconception in tennis. Sure, pros hit the ball hard, but they still use a speed they can control. TENNIS IS NOT A GAME OF POWER BUT AN APPROPRIATE OR INTELLIGENT USE OF SPEED!

A mature or well-trained player hits his "best shot." He doesn't hold back, but he also knows not to attempt a shot he cannot make. He knows how to play up to his ability but within his ability.

What is your best shot? It varies. It is again important for you to have an understanding of our variables — contact point, court position, and body position. It is crucial to read the variables on the court correctly, so you know whether the play controls your shot selection or whether you have alternatives.

If all three of the factors are in your favor and you have plenty of time, then you can probably direct your shot to any number of targets. You control the play. If the ball comes with such difficulty that all of the variables are not in your favor, then the play controls you.

If the play controls you, don't fight it. GO WITH THE FLOW! Do not fight the variables; work with them. Use them to your advantage to win the point. When a player understands the variables and works with them, he will not make many unforced errors. A GREAT NUMBER OF UNFORCED ERRORS ARE THE RESULT OF FIGHTING THE FLOW — poor choices — RATHER THAN BEING A POOR PLAYER. DO NOT BREAK THIS LAW! Go With the Flow! What are the different flows in a point? Here is a list:

1. The direction of the ball traveling toward you.
2. The direction of your shot.
3. The speed of your opponent's shot.
4. The speed of your shot.
5. The height over the net of your opponent's shot.
6. The height over the net of your shot.
7. Your footwork. The direction of your weight transfer at your contact point (the lower half of your body).
8. The direction of your swing (control of your upper body).
9. The implications of your contact point (high, low, in front, in back, etc.).
10. Amount of swing you take.

The idea is to hit your shot back changing as few of the flows as possible. Going from the known — staying in the

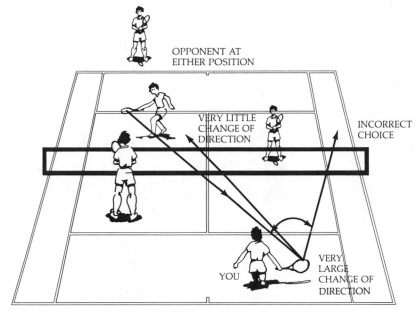

OPPONENT AT
EITHER POSITION

VERY LITTLE
CHANGE OF
DIRECTION

INCORRECT
CHOICE

VERY
LARGE
CHANGE OF
DIRECTION

YOU

DIAGRAM 33

flow — to the unknown — fighting or changing the flow — opens the potential for many more errors. The fewer changes that are made, the easier it is to control the ball.

The following diagrams and explanations should clarify how to Go With the Flow.

In Diagrams 33-36 these are constants:
1. You are on or just in front of the service line.
2. The ball is traveling at you from the deeper — on the service line or baseline — crosscourt opponent.
3. The other opponent is directly in front of you at the net.
   Diagram 33 variables:
1. Your contact is below the top of the net, because the ball came low over the net.
2. The ball is traveling at a medium speed.
3. Your weight transfer is toward the net.

Analysis. Because your contact point is low, you do not have the potential for a put-away. So, Go With the Flow. Send the ball back the same direction — deep to deep — and at the same height over the net. If you return it at the

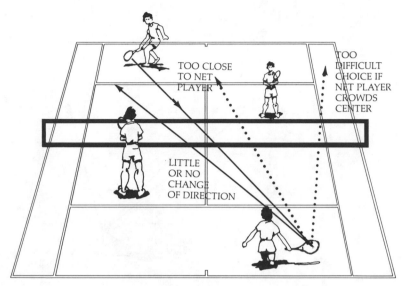

TOO CLOSE
TO NET
PLAYER

TOO
DIFFICULT
CHOICE IF
NET PLAYER
CROWDS
CENTER

LITTLE
OR NO
CHANGE
OF DIRECTION

DIAGRAM 34

same speed or slightly slower, you should be able to control the ball. Your weight is shifting toward the net, so your crosscourt return is consistent with your weight transfer.

Going for either alley would be fighting the flow. It would require a) a change in direction, b) a change in height to go over the highest point of the net, c) body adjustments in pointing the shoulders and stepping toward the target, and d) change in speed. If you did not slow the ball down, it would not have enough time to rise over the highest part of the net and fall back down into the court.

The risks of making an error when changing this many variables are not worth the gain. You are investing your effort and time during a tennis match. Make shrewd investments. Is the risk worth the gain?

Diagram 34 Variables:
1. Same low contact point.
2. Same medium speed.
3. Your weight transfer is still forward.
4. Difference — the shot toward you was hit at a sharper

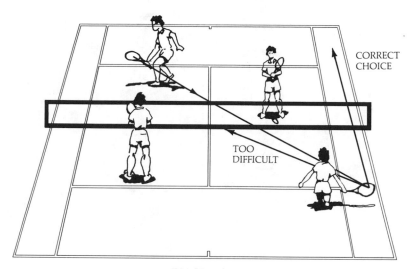

CORRECT
CHOICE

TOO
DIFFICULT

DIAGRAM 35

crosscourt angle. You are now standing nearer your alley
when you are hitting.

Analysis. You still do not have the potential to add pace to
your shot. The key difference is that you are pulled wider in
your court. Stay with the direction of the ball and return it
wider. A ball being hit down the center will pass too close
to the net player. Because your ball travels all the way
crosscourt, this should give you adequate time to recover
into good court position.

You could possibly aim the ball down the alley in front of
you. This would require a drastic change in direction to a
small target. Try it only when the net player has left her
alley open or if you have superb racquet control.

Diagram 35 Variables:

1. Same low contact point.
2. Same speed of ball approaching you.
3. You are pulled wide as in Diagram 34 or wider.
4. Difference. This time the ball has gotten behind you into
   the alley, so you are forced to step sideways — parallel

PERMISSIBLE
TO CHANGE
DIRECTION

DIAGRAM 36

to the net — to reach the shot.

Analysis. A crosscourt shot came at you, so it is desirable to return your shot crosscourt to stay with the flow. The overriding or dominant flow, though, is your last step. This is in the opposite direction from which the ball came toward you. Hitting back crosscourt in this situation would force your upper body to twist crosscourt while your lower half is stepping toward the sideline. It is more important to maintain the flow of the body —both halves of the body working together — than it is to hit the ball back in the same direction from which it came. Allow the strongest flow to dictate your shot selection. It is crucial to understand that in certain situations one must change one flow in order to preserve a more important flow. It is also important to understand this is more difficult to execute than when all the flows are working together. Take this into consideration in your shot selection. In this particular situation, you would take pace off your shot for control. It should also stay lower over the net. Aim at the alley in front of you, working with the flow of your body.

Diagram 36 Variables.

1. Same crosscourt shot.
2. Same medium speed.
3. Your weight transfer is forward and under control.
4. Difference. Your contact point is now eye level.

Analysis. Finally, it is going your way. Here you have excellent court position, excellent balance, and now a perfect contact point. All three factors are in your favor. You should be able to change the flow and not risk an error.

Change the direction. Take the crosscourt shot and aim your put-away at the net person in front of you. He should not have time to react.

Do not get greedy. Do not change too many flows. For example, changing the speed — adding more speed — could risk overhitting into an error. Also, hard balls travel in a straight line. Your shot could stay too high, giving your opponent an easier contact point.

Obviously, we could fill hundreds of pages listing every potential situation that could occur in a match. That is not possible, nor is it necessary if you can analyze the variables and flows.

In the four diagrams, Diagram 33 was the model; Diagram 34 changed the direction of the ball; Diagram 35 changed the direction of your footwork; and Diagram 36 changed the contact point. Changing one factor resulted in different shot selections. This is probably the most difficult concept for an intermediate player to grasp. In football, whoever has the ball is definitely on offense, and the player trying to get the ball is definitely on defense. This may not change for six or eight minutes at a time while a team is driving down the field. In baseball, there is no question who is batting and who is fielding. Changing one variable in tennis, however, can change the entire personality of the point. Whether you are in charge of the point or in trouble could conceivably change with every hit. This happens very quickly. It requires intense concentration and numerous practice sessions to perfect your observation skills and to train your body to move fast enough.

Study your shots. Learn to Go With the Flow. Take the easy way out. Develop the point until your opponent eventually must fight the flow to get the ball back in. This will result in his error or his inability to hit a strong shot.

On the court
1. Play games. Refer to the list of flows. Play points where everyone tries to choose targets that stay in the flow. Emphasize one flow on each point and go through the list.
2. Between points of practice matches, talk to your partner. Analyze each point and see if you stayed with the flow.
3. Play out points. Winning the point scores one credit. Losing the point scores nothing. Losing the point by fighting the flow receives a minus one. Switch servers when one team gets to five.

Positive self-talk
1. I try to Go With the Flow when I play. I send the ball back at a similar speed, angle, height over the net, etc.
2. I change the flow only when I am forced to because several variables are against me, or when I choose to because all the variables are with me. I have time to recognize this.

Moving violations: charging the net

Your ultimate goal is to control the net as a team. Both you and your partner should be in front of The Most Important Line on the Court. Both of you will then have the potential to win the point. More important than your ability to put the ball away is that your opponents must hit a perfect shot to beat you. It requires perfect placement for them to hit a passing shot through both of you or place a lob deep enough so that you cannot run after and retrieve it. Make them be perfect to beat you.

All points begin with only one player, the server's partner, at the net. The other three players must move forward to obtain a good position at the net.

Most players, as they move into the net, keep moving through their volley. THIS CAUSES A GREAT NUMBER OF ERRORS! The problem is not lack of skill but lack of stability — poor body control at contact point! Because your responsibility is to cover only one-half of the court, there is sufficient time to get set for most volleys. Only a spectacular shot by your opponent will force you to be lunging at contact. The key to rushing the net and being stable on the volley is to execute The Rhythm Method of

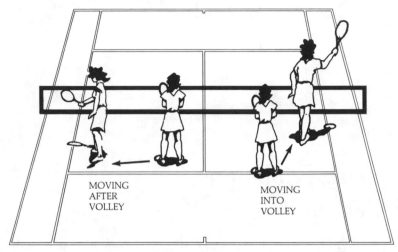

MOVING AFTER VOLLEY

MOVING INTO VOLLEY

DIAGRAM 37

Ball Control correctly. Hit your serve, service return, or approach shot; then move in as fast and as far as you can. When your ball bounces on the other side or when your opponent begins to swing her racquet forward, come to a relaxed, soft-landing, split-step stop.

Stopping the split-second before your opponent makes contact means that you are ready to adjust in any fashion. You are making constructive movement toward the ball the first instant you recognize where it is traveling. Stopping late means you will be late! You may also make some destructive movement — still moving forward when you should be moving sideways or backwards.

Here is the key point of this chapter. Stopping, being tuned into the rhythm, allows adequate time to read the ball, adjust (move) for it, and have good timing on the volley. (Remember, timing is having your body and racquet travel in the same direction at contact.)

You should be able to move into the volley in a V fashion instead of moving AFTER the ball in a T fashion (Diagram

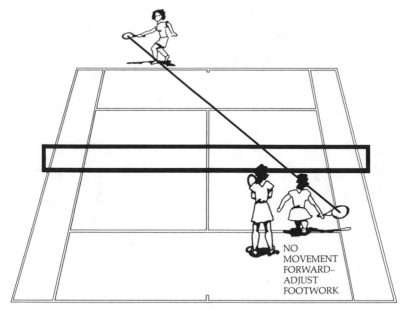

NO
MOVEMENT
FORWARD–
ADJUST
FOOTWORK

DIAGRAM 38A

37). Lunging after the ball in a T fashion should only
happen when your opponent hits a spectacular shot. Give
her credit. Go on and win the next point.

Rushing the net and volleying are relatively easy if you
have time to move into your volleys in a V fashion. The
next step is to be able to read the speed of the ball and its
height over the net. This will tell you how much court you
can cover.

A ball that travels low over the net and very fast does
not allow for time to move in. Instead, use the time that
stopping early has given you and adjust your feet to
establish a crossover step and a contact point in front of
your body. A stable or stationary racquet head would also
be required. It would be impractical to swing at a ball
where your contact point is so low. (See Diagram 38,
Example A.) You are content to get down and ready. You
would not be able to move in. Remember that "balls hit
hard travel in a straight line." You will also be required to
take some pace off this shot. Hit it back easily. Go for

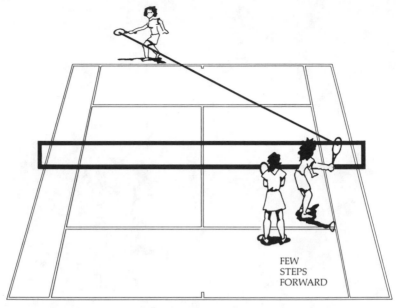

FEW
STEPS
FORWARD

DIAGRAM 38B

placement, not power.

If a ball comes over the net a little higher and slower, you have time to move in. Move in a couple of steps, but just before contact, make your crossover step and hit the volley in a stable position (Example B).

THERE IS NO SUCH THING AS AN EASY BALL! The ball is floating softly and with good height over the net in Example C. But do not swing at it because it is higher; extra power from a swing is not necessary. And do not think you can be casual and run through it because it is a slower ball. Run several steps forward for this ball. Time your movement so you can stop and then hit it at the peak or at the highest comfortable contact point for you. Accurate placement from stopping and blocking will produce a winner. Extra swinging and extra movement lead only to extra errors.

It is true, though, that life is not perfect. Sometimes it may be advantageous to be hitting the volley on the run in order to catch it above the net or achieve an easier contact

SEVERAL
STEPS
FORWARD

DIAGRAM 38C

point. This is fine. Just be aware that less body control leads
to less ball control. Do not try to do as much with your
shot. Place it; don't power it.

You are rushing in most often behind a serve or a return.
Many players are taught they must serve and get to the
service line, plant, and volley. THIS IS A MYTH; ONE
CANNOT BE SO RIGID. Factors such as the speed of your
serve, position of the receiver on the court, and your foot
speed will all vary. Tune into the rhythm of the play, not a
line on the court. There is a great deal of adjusting to be
done after your split-step stop. It should be clear that here is
where most of the work is done — adjustments after the
split-step stop. Do not try to run in so far that you do not
leave adequate time to read the variables and adjust to
them. This makes a player late and lunging at contact point.
Be mentally prepared to hit a minimum of three shots each
time you charge the net — a serve (or return), a first volley
(set-up shot), and a second volley (put-away shot). A good
opponent will not let you win many points with hitting just

two shots.

On the court

1. Work one on one. Drop a ball, hit it, and move toward the net. Stop when the ball bounces on the other side. Your split-step stop should be a soft landing. Keep hovering; do not plant too firmly.

2. Do the same as in Number 1. The opponent now hits your ball back. Read the variables, move into the ball, and volley it. HOLD YOUR FINISH AT CONTACT. Are you stable? Were you able to move into your volley in a V fashion? Do not play out the point.

3. Do the same as in Number 2, but now play the point out. Keep working your way toward the net, stopping properly each time your opponent makes contact with the ball.

4. Do the same as in Number 3. Now use one ball for all four players. This time your opponents move in after they hit. Notice as all four of you get closer and closer to the net, you have less and less time between each shot. Stop sooner and sooner.

5. Here's an excellent drill, one of the key practice routines. Stand on the service line. Your hitting partner stands crosscourt on the baseline. She aims her shots at your feet. You read the ball coming at you. If it is low, get down. If it is high, move in for it. (Remember to stop before you hit.) Baseline player works on hitting the feet. Service line player works on ball judgment skills and movement while trying to land her shots deep in the court.

6. Hit a serve and move in. Watch your serve going over the net. Do your split-step stop when your opponent starts her swing. Hold your position. Are you stable?.

7. Repeat Number 6. Now move into your volley, hit it, and hold your finish. Are you stable and balanced?

8. Repeat Number 7 and play out the point.

9. Repeat Number 6 through 8 as a receiver.

Positive self-talk

1. I have a good sense of rhythm. I come to a split-step stop when my ball bounces on the other side or when I see my opponent's racquet start to move.
2. I read the ball coming at me and know how much court I can cover.
3. I am able to move INTO most of my volleys. I AM NOT CAUGHT MOVING AFTER MY VOLLEYS.
4. I am stable and balanced when I volley. I do not commit very many unforced errors.

The lethal lob and the overhead

Have you often heard the remark, "We lost, but it wasn't real tennis. They lobbed a lot!"? Is it true that real men do not eat quiche, and good tennis players do not lob? I cannot comment with authority on the eating habits of macho men, but I do know that the lob is an essential shot for a complete tennis game.

There are two kinds of lobs: defensive and offensive. A defensive lob is hit high over the net. You may have poor court position, or an awkward contact point, or your opponents may be very close to the net. You lob to buy time to recover or to move your opponents from the net. You are not concerned about putting the ball away.

An offensive lob is placed just above the reach of the net players. They will not have time to run after the ball and return it. An offensive lob may be difficult for an interme- diate player to execute.

Two ideas are important to remember when executing a lob. First, stroke a lob like any other ground stroke. Do not alter your stroke pattern. It is too difficult to have different stroke patterns for every type of shot. Changing your stroke also alerts your opponent to your intentions. Slightly open

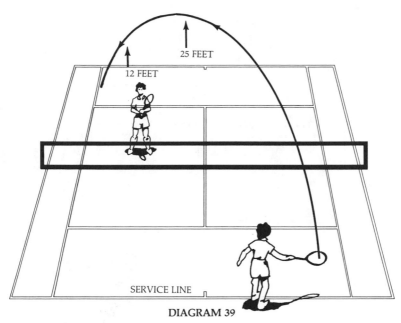

25 FEET

12 FEET

SERVICE LINE

DIAGRAM 39

your racquet face at contact to achieve a lob. Second,
HAVE A TARGET! This is crucial for successful lobbing!
Take a mental picture of a spot twenty-five feet above the
net and imagine a twelve-foot high wall on the service line.
Your lob should hit this spot over the net and clear the wall
on the service line. (See Diagram 39.) Hit these targets, and
your lobbing will be successful. It will be irrelevant how tall
your opponent is.

Lob when you are pulled off the court — far behind the
baseline or wide of the doubles sideline. Time is needed to
get back into a good tactical position. Lob when you have
an awkward contact point or poor balance. Take the easy
way out — do not force a shot by a net player or into a
small section of the court. The risk is not worth the gain.

Lob when your opponents have control of the net. They
are well in front of The Most Important Line on the Court.
It is too difficult to get the ball down at their feet. Try to
pass them only when all three variables are in your favor.

It is important to read the effect your lob has on your

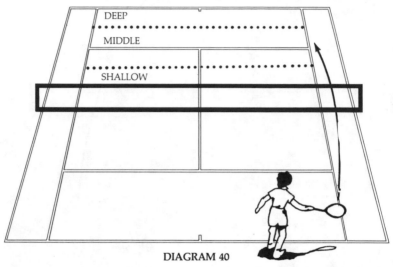

DIAGRAM 40

opponents and to adjust your court position accordingly. Divide your opponents' court into three zones — shallow, middle, and deep. (See Diagram 40.)

There is very little time to react when you hit a shallow lob. Read your opponents' body language. Observe the direction their feet point, the way their shoulders are turned, and the direction of their stroke pattern. Run to the spot where you think they will be hitting their shot just before their contact with the ball. If you anticipate correctly, you may be able to save the point. Obviously, block another lob, hoping to get into the point.

You and your partner should shift toward the opposite side of the court from the hitter when the lob places the opponents in the middle zone. (See Diagram 41.) Place your left foot behind the center service mark. Your partner puts his left foot behind the singles sideline. The purpose is to have you and your partner cover two holes — the center and the long crosscourt diagonal. Force your opponent to hit to the shortest corner and smallest target, the alley in

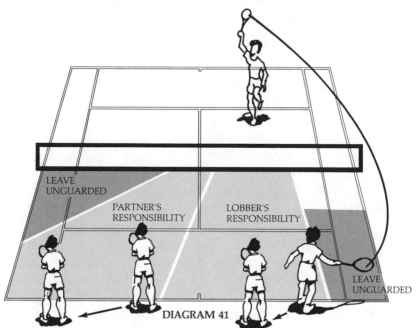

LEAVE
UNGUARDED

PARTNER'S
RESPONSIBILITY

LOBBER'S
RESPONSIBILITY

LEAVE
UNGUARDED

DIAGRAM 41

front of him. This is difficult to do from the middle zone.
Make your opponents prove they can do it before you
guard the smallest target. If they hit this target successfully
two or three times, then shift that way and guard it. Make
your opponent change his target. Move at a 45-degree angle
backward as you shift. This will get you five or six feet
behind the baseline. This extra distance will allow you to
handle deep and very hard-hit overheads more easily.

Assuming your opponents were standing in front of The
Most Important Line on the Court when you lobbed, they
will not hit an overhead from the deep zone with authority.
This is a long distance to run to get a lob. Most intermediate to advanced players will let the ball bounce or hit it at
one-half speed. When you do hit a good deep lob, read
how your opponents are handling the shot. If they look
awkward, will be late to reach the ball, or will let it bounce,
charge the net. Your opponents should not be able to hit a
winner after they have scrambled after your good lob. You
should be at the net for the chance to put the ball away. If

your opponents were standing on the service line or are top-notch players, they may be able to handle your deep lob. Again the key is to read the variables! Shift as though the lob landed in the middle zone if they handle deep lobs well.

There will be occasions when you are on the service line, and your partner on the baseline lobs. When your partner lobs to the shallow or middle zone, backpedal (or run) as fast and as far as you can. STOP when your opponent's racquet starts to move and get set for the oncoming overhead. Crouch down like a hockey goalie; give your opponent a smaller target. Balls passing you chest-high or higher will be long. You need only guard balls that pass by you low. You can charge toward the net if your partner successfully lobs into the deep zone — assuming your opponent looks awkward. The baseline player would do the same movements as explained previously. His partner's being on the service line would not affect his movements.

NOTICE WHEN YOUR LOB IS TAKEN ON THE BACKHAND SIDE. Intermediate and even some advanced players cannot run backwards and hit a high backhand volley with power. They may not miss it, but they cannot smash it. Charge! Get into the net and put away that ball floating softly back at you. Not attacking here loses a golden opportunity for success.

Professional players can stand right on top of the net and are still quick enough to cover the deepest lob. But it is difficult to coax club players to get really close to the net for the put-away. They complain, "All I do is get lobbed." It is frustrating to watch teams stand far away from the net to protect themselves from being lobbed: they never are in position to put the ball away. A good compromise for the intermediate to advanced team is the LETHAL LOB play.

You have just lobbed your service return over the head of the server's partner. (See Diagram 42.) Your partner, being closer to the net, plays navel tennis and straddles the center service line. There is nothing illegal or immoral about stepping on your partner's side of the court. Since your partner is roughly in the center of the court, the server

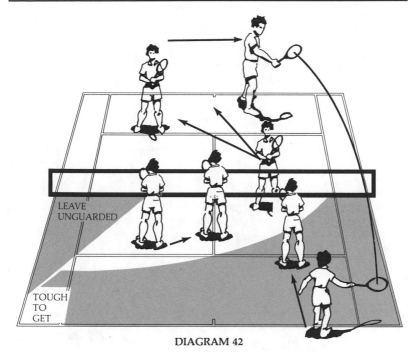

DIAGRAM 42

cannot run crosscourt after the lob and blast a crosscourt passing shot. Give that shot away. Also give him the passing shot into the alley. Your partner virtually covers the entire net by standing in the center of the court. The receiver's partner can put away any easy floater because he is there waiting so close to the net.

Move toward the net after you see that your lob has cleared the server's partner, and stop on the service line. Your partner has the net covered, so you can stay back on the service line as a safety valve to cover a lob from the server. The server must lob crosscourt into a tiny five-square-foot area to really hurt the receiving team. (See Diagram 42.) This is why the play is so lethal!

Some teaching pros will argue this is not correct doubles positioning. For a professional level of play, it is not. But for club-level play, it covers both worlds — closing off the net and defending against the lob.

It is important to read how your opponent is handling your lob. If your lob is not spectacular — landing in the

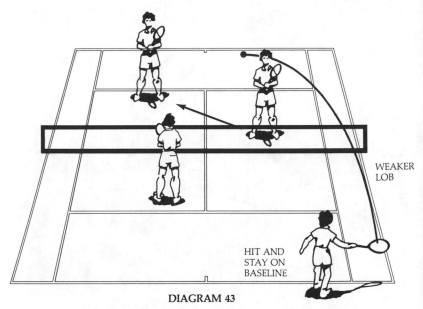

WEAKER
LOB

HIT AND
STAY ON
BASELINE

DIAGRAM 43

center of the court or shorter — then your opponent is not as stressed. Do not be as aggressive. The lobber may stay on the baseline. (See Diagram 43.) If the lob puts tremendous pressure on your opponent, then be very aggressive. (See Diagram 44.) The receiver's partner can cross over more, and the receiver can switch. The receiver's partner would expect to pick off almost all shots.

Now for a few words about overheads.

Do not swing at every overhead. When all the variables are in your favor, you can hit the overhead. When you are awkward or have a poor contact point, block the ball. You should be able to return any lob this way.

Decide early to run or shuffle. If the lob is in the shallow or middle zone, you may be able to shuffle back and hit the overhead. When the lob carries toward the deep zone, a player cannot cover enough court fast enough by shuffling. Turn your feet toward the back screen and run back. Whichever the lob, do not move backwards with your navel facing toward the net. This is too slow and dangerous.

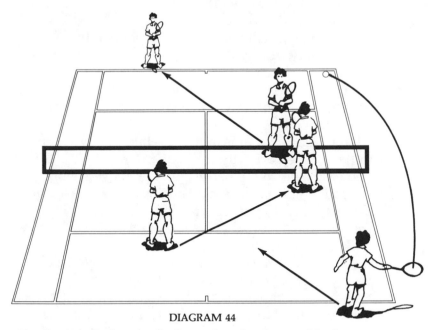

DIAGRAM 44

Professional players find overheads easy to hit, but most club players find them difficult. A great deal of the difference is that professional players can set up a good contact point and have a good sense of rhythm. Pointing your non-racquet hand at the ball will assist in the improvement of both of these concepts. Pretend you can catch the ball in your non-racquet hand. You will have set up the perfect contact point if you can catch the ball out in front of you. Pointing this hand in the air should also create a better sense of depth perception: it should be clearer when to swing.

Remember deep to deep and close to close. When you have control of your overhead smash, aim at the closer person or into the open court. Direct your overhead toward the farther opponent when you do not have the potential to put the ball away.

On the court
1. Have a friend toss balls to you. Practice stroking a lob.

Aim for a target above the net. Make adjustments necessary to groove your lob.

2. Do the same as Number 1. Now have him feed balls farther away from you, so you must hit your lob on the run.
3. Do the same as Number 1, but have him feed very fast balls at you. Shorten your swing accordingly. Practice blocking a lob.
4. All four players stand on the baseline. Lob your shots to them. They drive the ball back.
5. Lob easy balls to the net player. Net players work on the ball judgment skills by catching lobs in their non-racquet hand. Catch ten, then hit them.
6. Feed middle-depth lobs. Net players work on shuffling back for overheads.
7. Feed deep lobs. Net players run back for overheads. Swing or block overheads where appropriate.
8. Stand on the baseline and hit easy lobs to a net player. Your partner stands on the service line. Net player hits overhead at service line player. You and your partner work on moving back and shifting.
9. Same positions as Number 8. Feed a deep lob. You and your partner work on moving in.
10. Place two opponents at the net. You and your partner stand on the baseline. Feed shallow, middle, and deep lobs. Shift and move properly.
11. Opponents serve. Hit a lob return. If lob is deep enough, move into the LETHAL LOB play.

Positive self-talk
1. I am relaxed when I lob.
2. I stroke my lob when I can and block it when I must.
3. I always aim for a target when I lob.
4. I have good ball judgment skills on my overheads.
5. I know when to block my overheads and when to swing at them.
6. I know when to shuffle back and when to run back for overheads.

7. My partner and I shift properly when we lob. We recognize the ability of our opponents when they are hitting their shots.
8. My partner and I can execute the LETHAL LOB play.

Democrat or Republican: the art of poaching

We have discussed the need for discipline in order to eliminate unforced errors. It is a shame, though, not to be aggressive and to let balls go by that could have been reached and probably put away.

When you poach, your goal is to put the ball away. A player must know which balls can be picked off, and which balls would be futile to chase. This is the politics of poaching: which balls you can move after in a conservative or Republican fashion, and which balls permit more liberal or Democratic movement.

THE KEY IN INTELLIGENT POACHING IS TO BE ABLE TO READ THE THREE VARIABLES IN YOUR OPPONENTS BEFORE THEY MAKE CONTACT WITH THE BALL. When your opponents are not stressed, in other words when all three variables are in their favor, do not attempt to move around or poach. Because the ball is so easy for them, they could hit to several different targets. Your job is to guard your own section of the court. Do not expect to get all balls. Picking off these balls would require your reaction and then movement *after* your opponents hit the ball.

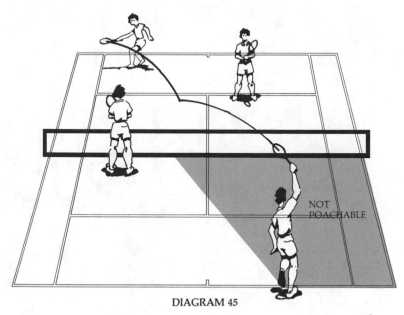

NOT
POACHABLE

DIAGRAM 45

Republican Poaching. Use conservative movement when your opponents have some limitations in their shot. You can move slightly — before they make contact with the ball. Of our three variables only one or at the most two variables are in the disfavor of your opponent. You can leave some court open because it would be almost impossible for them to thread the needle behind you. Republican poaching is slight movement before your opponent makes contact with the ball and then a reaction to the shot.

Democratic Poaching. Sometimes, all three variable are awkward for your opponent. Because you see your opponent in such trouble, you are free to leave a great section of the court open. You know he cannot fight the flow. Move before your opponent makes contact with the ball, so you have time to cover the required court distance and intercept his shot.

Here are three diagrams illustrating poaching as seen through the eyes of the server's partner.

Diagram 45 variables:

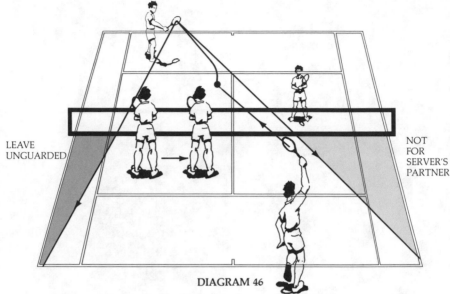

LEAVE
UNGUARDED

NOT
FOR
SERVER'S
PARTNER

DIAGRAM 46

1. The serve lands shallow in the service court.
2. The serve lands in the center of the service court.
3. The serve is slow.
4. The person is hitting the ball on the alley side of his
   body.

Analysis. All the factors are in the favor of the receiver. It
would be foolish to poach off such a serve. Get ready and
defend your own territory. It is difficult to run down shots
that angle crosscourt away from you.

   Diagram 46 variables:

1. The serve lands deeper in the service court.
2. The serve is medium speed.
3. The person is hitting the ball with his backhand.
4. The service still lands in the center of the service court.

Analysis. This is a Republican poach. A deeper serve going
to the backhand makes it more difficult for your opponent
to hit your alley. Some conservative movement into the
center of the court is appropriate. Move the proportionate
distance over that you believe your opponent can no longer

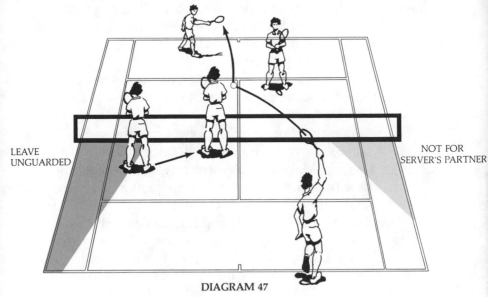

LEAVE
UNGUARDED

NOT FOR
SERVER'S PARTNER

DIAGRAM 47

hit into. Playing navel tennis should be your guide.
   Diagram 47 variables:
1. The serve lands deep in the service court.
2. The serve is faster.
3. The serve is in the corner of the service court, near the
   center T.
4. The receiver has to step sideways to reach the ball and
   makes contact slightly late.
Analysis. Gangbusters! This is a Democratic poach. All the
variables place the opponent in trouble and indicate a return
through the center. Move quickly to cover the center.
Notice that because you have moved over considerably,
your target shifts over as well to keep the ball away from
the receiver.
   If you read the variables correctly, you should be able to
know when to guard your alley and when to leave it open
and poach. Of course, there are always some other possibil-
ities. You can misread the play; your opponent can hit a
lucky shot; or he can be a level better as a player than you

thought. A shot you think would be difficult for an opponent may not be. Do not feel bad about being burned down your alley once or twice. If it doesn't happen that often, then you aren't being aggressive enough. If it happens more often, then be more conservative.

Here are some extra ideas:

1. Poach for surprise. You may try an aggressive movement even though your opponent isn't terribly stressed to catch him by surprise.
2. Poach a favorite shot. If an opponent hits the same predictable shot, move a little early once and pick it off.
3. Fake a poach. Make a movement toward the center and then come back just before your opponent hits, trying to sucker him into hitting into your alley.
4. Many times you will poach and hit the ball while you are still moving. This is acceptable. Keep the racquet head stable, though. The force of your body moving will supply enough energy. Swinging can only lead to mishitting.
5. Your movement should be at a 45-degree angle forward when poaching so as to cut off the ball earlier and be guaranteed of a higher contact point. See Diagram 47.

On the court

1. Play the position of the server's partner. Depending on how the serve lands, stand still or make a Democratic or Republican poach.
2. Have someone serve all balls for the center T. Work on aggressive poaching.
3. Have your partner serve balls at the center T. Work on poaching movements at a 45-degree angle forward.
4. Have your partner serve. When poaching, work on holding the racquet head still at contact point. No swings.
5. Repeat Drills 2-4 with you at the net and a feeder on the baseline directly in front of you. He feeds balls through the middle of the court, and you work on your skills.

Positive self-talk

1. I am aware when a ball lands in front of my opponent whether I should guard my section of the court, leave some unguarded, or poach aggressively. I can read this before he makes contact with the shot.
2. I move forward at a 45-degree angle when I poach.
3. I hold my racquet head stable when hitting the ball on my poach.
4. I am developing a sixth sense when to poach on a sneak attack.
5. I am getting faster and faster at reading the opportunity for a poach.

Dial-a-mate

As a net player, you may like your partner on the baseline, but you cannot always trust her. An opposing net player may pick off one of her shots. For this reason, your ATTENTION should be directed at the opposing net player when a ball travels from behind you. You may glance back at your partner to anticipate her shot or to see if she has tripped over the baseline while she is stroking the ball. But make this a quick look; direct the major focus of your attention at the first person who will be hitting a ball at you, the opposing net player.

When the receiver hits her return to the server's partner, the receiver realizes she has very little time to react. As you can see in Diagram 48, the receiver anticipates that server's partner will aim for the center and moves there ahead of server's partner's contact.

The receiver's partner realizes there is no time to back up, so gets down like a hockey goalie ready for the ball at her feet.

The server's partner should aim the ball to pass by the receiver's partner's feet. Do not give her a chance to hit your shot. Aim for the center T.

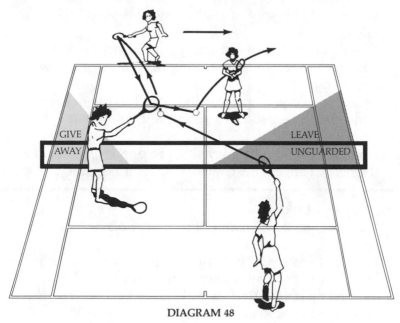

DIAGRAM 48

The server realizes her partner has a shot with a good contact point and moves toward the net in case the receiver's partner or the receiver would get the ball back. THIS IS CRUCIAL. Do not assume your partner will automatically put the ball away. Keep moving toward the net until your opponent makes contact with her shot. (Remember the Rhythm Method.) Both you and your partner will be near the net. There is no opening for your opponents to get back into the point.

If your partner consistently hits balls to the net player, collect your racquet and valuables, go to the nearest telephone, and "Dial for a new Mate or Partner!"

On the court

1. Be aware of which opponent is hitting the ball. Say "deep" to yourself when the opponent farther away from you is hitting the ball, or say "close" when the opponent closer to you is hitting the ball. Make the proper movement depending on which person hits the ball.

2. When you hit a ball to a net person, anticipate and run to the probable spot of her put-away attempt before she hits it.
3. When you are at the net and your partner behind you hits an easy ball to an opposing net player, get down and ready.
4. When you or your partner hits a ball to the net player, remember where she tries to put it away. What is her favorite target?
5. Analyze why you hit easy shots to opposing players at the net. Change your choice of shots if necessary.

Positive self-talk

1. I can recognize when an opposing net player has an easy shot.
2. I realize I have very little time to react, and I anticipate before my opponent makes contact with the shot. Depending on the time available, I get down and ready or run to the probable target.
3. I remember my opponents' tendencies and anticipate correctly the majority of times!
4. When I am deep and an easy ball goes to my partner, I move in to the net in case our opponents get it back.

Legalized cheating: how to anticipate

If you have mastered the previous chapters, then you realize that there are a number of concepts that follow common-sense logic. The flurry of balls traveling back and forth over the net can be broken down into logical parts.

One can recognize the same patterns happening time and time again. Once these basic ideas are easily understood during a point, the awareness of a player can be expanded to observe more variables. It is eventually possible to be so sensitive to all of the variables and options present on the court that a player can logically understand what can or must happen one or several shots ahead of time. This ability to predict the future correctly is called anticipation.

The benefit of anticipation is that it frees a player to move to the place where the ball is going before the opponent has hit it. This is such a phenomenal advantage it's almost too good to be true. It's almost like cheating, but it is not. Anticipation is legal!

There is no question that the amount of court you can cover determines your level of play! THIS POINT CANNOT BE OVERSTATED! How many balls you can run down places you in your level of play more than any other factor in tennis.

There are two ways to increase your court coverage. One is to give up chocolates and exercise fanatically! A better diet and improved strength will make you faster.

The other way is through improved anticipation, more movement when you are not hitting the ball. Everyone knows to run toward the ball when you are about to hit it. Unfortunately, most players hit and then stand after they hit it.

Think of a basketball game. Do nine players stand and watch one person dribble? Or in hockey, do all the players stand with their chins on their sticks as one lone person skates around freely with the puck? Of course not! Watch your friends play doubles, though, and see how three players stand and watch the fourth one hitting. More and more purposeful movement when you don't have the ball is critical to improvement!

One must be sensitive in order to have good anticipation. Feel, see, and hear how the ball left your racquet and make logical deductions. If the shot you made felt and looked fantastic, then anticipate that a weak shot will come back. Likewise, if you hit a poor shot, anticipate a strong return.

Combine this with sensitivity to your opponent's play. How does he look at his contact point? Where is his contact point? Ankle high or chest high? How is his balance? Is he tripping over the service line or firmly planted? Where is he standing on the court? Is he two feet from the net and salivating or five feet behind the baseline and trembling? Being aware of these factors will easily tell you the potential and limitations of his return shot.

Now that you have a pretty good idea of where he will hit, you can do two things. One, move to that spot immediately. If you are there earlier, the next shot should be easier to hit. Two, you can leave a section of the court unguarded, because you know he cannot or would not try to aim there.

Don't be misled that anticipation is always dramatic or covering huge amounts of court. It could be as simple as

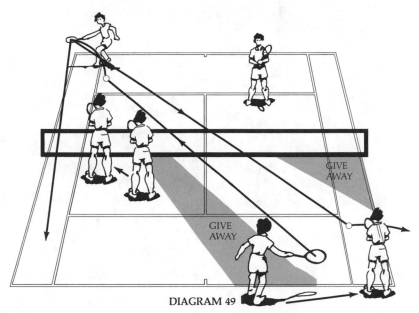

DIAGRAM 49

hitting a ground stroke from the middle of no man's land and realizing it was not strong enough to follow into the net. Anticipate that a ground stroke will come back. Your job would be then to hit and move behind the baseline. Most players hit, then stand in no man's land only to get a ball at their feet, which is awkward to return.

Try to do most of your movement when the ball leaves your racquet or your partner's and travels to your opponent. When your opponent hits it, then you will not have that much work left to do as the ball travels toward you.

A phrase worth committing to memory and gaining an understanding of is "Balls that go over wide, come back wide. Balls that go through the center, come back through the center."

In Diagram 49, notice how your opponent is wide in the alley. Remember our rule — balls that go over wide, come back wide. Anticipate this. Your net partner should shift to his left to cover the wide ball down his alley. You on the baseline should shift to your right to cover the sharp

LEAVE
UNGUARDE

DIAGRAM 50

crosscourt coming back wide. If you stay in the middle of
your half, it would be difficult to reach the sharp crosscourt
ground stroke. The shot down the center between the two
of you is the most difficult winner for your opponent to hit.
THIS IS THE ONE TIME THAT YOU AND YOUR
PARTNER SPLIT IN OPPOSITE DIRECTIONS.

In Diagram 50, you are at the net with your partner.
Your partner still covers his alley. You shift with your
partner and guard the center; because you are so close to
the net, your opponent would have to hit an extremely
good crosscourt to beat you.

In Diagram 51, your opponent is in the center of the
court. The net player shifts to the center (navel tennis). You
on the baseline can shift to the right also, because your
partner has the middle covered. It should be no problem to
run after a ball lobbed over your partner's head.

In Diagram 52, you have volleyed down the center, so
both of you can converge in a V toward the center. It
would be difficult for your opponents to make your alleys.

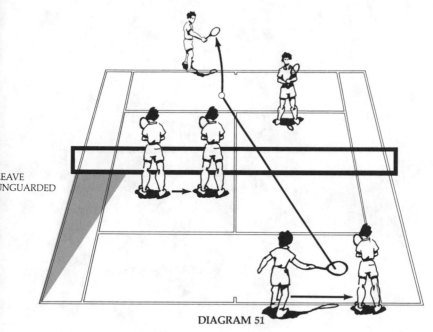

LEAVE
UNGUARDED

DIAGRAM 51

These examples illustrate that an opponent can place his shot into three general target areas — either alley or through the center. Since there are just two of you, you and your partner must decide which are the two easier targets for your opponent to try for. Move into position to protect or "cover" those two openings, and leave unguarded the third opening. This opening should be the lowest percentage shot. Don't worry about your opponent's trying this shot; he will miss it many more times than he will make it.

Giving away one-third of your side of the court allows for easy coverage of the other two-thirds. This builds toward playing two on one — you and your partner in excellent court position playing against or ganging up on one opponent.

Move to these spots as the ball travels to your opponents, so you can be waiting for their next shot! This concept of anticipation and "movement without the ball" is probably the single biggest factor that lifts anyone from an intermediate to an advanced player.

DIAGRAM 52

On the court

1. Watch your opponent. Observe the variables in his
   contact point.
   a. Is he stable or moving as he is hitting?
   b. Is his contact point good or awkward?
   c. Which way are his feet, shoulders, and racquet face
   pointing at contact?
   d. Is he standing wide or in the center of his court?
   e. Add to this with your own ideas. Play out points. Do
   not keep track of the score. Work on your reading skills.
2. Now that you can observe a-d in Number 1, try to
   predict what kind of shot will come back. Notice if "balls
   that go through the center come back through the center,
   and balls that go over wide come back wide" rule
   applies?
3. Play out points. Work on increasing your movement
   after your shot. Hit and move to the proper spot. Do
   not hit and stand.

4. Play out points. Try to anticipate what type shot will come back. How often do you anticipate correctly?

Positive self-talk
1. I am aware of what my opponent looks like at his contact point.
2. I am aware of what my opponent looks like just before his contact point.
3. I am able to anticipate what the potential and limitations are of my opponents' shots.
4. I am able to anticipate my opponents' shots and move. I do a lot of my movement while the ball is traveling to my opponent instead of waiting to do all of my movement as the ball is returning.
5. I have arrived as a doubles player. I can tell what will happen two or three shots ahead of time.

Let's play

Throughout the book we have dissected a tennis point into specific parts. By now, you should be able to recognize them and execute the desired shots. Playing the game in this logical manner — selecting the high-percentage shot — is your strategy. This should result in a victory for you. If not, then you have to know how to change your tactics so you can come out on top.

Your strategy and tactics must also be tailored to your level of play. Understand your strengths and weaknesses, and know what shots you can make in each situation. Reading the three variables will tell you which shot you should attempt.

The foundation of a good strategy is to know how not to lose. Be consistent. Consistency is defined as the elimination of unforced errors. Consistency always wins at its own level. THE EASIEST SOURCE AND GREATEST SOURCE OF POINTS IN ANY MATCH WILL COME FROM YOUR OPPONENTS' UNFORCED ERRORS. Let them self-destruct first. If this sounds too boring to you, then you are not a mature player yet.

Accuracy, the ability to be consistent to a smaller target,

comes next. Controlled placement to a designated area on the court (usually the feet of your opponent) will keep you in the point until there is an opportunity to win it.

Hitting winners comes last! This will make up the fewest number of points won. Therefore, YOUR GREATEST AND MOST RAPID IMPROVEMENT WILL COME FROM THE ELIMINATION OF UNFORCED ERRORS!

Now that you know how not to lose, let's talk about how to win. In addition to simply allowing your opponents to beat themselves, you must force them into errors. This is accomplished with aggressive movement, use of court position, and excellent shot placement. Hit and cover. (Remember movement without the ball.) Anticipate where the return shot is going and move to that spot. Place the ball perfectly to force a weak return. Move to the proper spot when you are not engaged in hitting.

Be there waiting to place the ball to the proper target. This is how you win matches — movement without the ball! Placement to the feet!

No two points are the same, and no two matches are the same. A blend of consistency with aggressive play will be required for optimum success.

Never change a winning strategy. Do not be more aggressive or play it safer in the second set after you have won the first set.

When you are losing, however, you must pull the proper solution out of your bag of tricks. Change your tactics. Don't play harder, play smarter. Do not wait until the last game. Change your tactics early enough that they can have an effect on the match. It may take some time for a change in tactics to have an effect.

There is no one answer to why someone loses a match. There could be several reasons. Different opponents have different weaknesses. Some detective work may be needed during a match. Here is an option list to refer to:

PROBLEM: OPTIONS:

They are more   A. Become more consistent.
consistent.
                            1. Concentrate better. Focus on the
                               ball. Block out all other
                               thoughts.
                            2. Always pick a target.
                            3. Go for a shot you know you can
                               make.
                            4. Lob a lot.

                        B. Become more aggressive.

                            1. Charge the net. Make them hit a
                               perfect passing shot or lob to
                               beat you.
                            2. Keep your ball at their feet.

                        C. Change your tactics.

                            1. Come to the net more.
                            2. Stay back more (probably not a
                               good choice if they are very
                               steady).
                            3. Change the rhythm. Hit your
                               ball at a different speed and a
                               different height over the net. Mix
                               up your shots. Try to destroy
                               their rhythm.
                            4. Bring them up to the net (may
                               be risky).
                            5. Be more patient. Wait for the
                               easy ball before you attempt a
                               put-away. Don't self-destruct.

You are erratic.   A. Concentrate better. Focus on the
                           ball.
                        B. Try for a higher percentage shot.
                        C. Calm down. Stop and set earlier. Be
                           more balanced while you are
                           hitting.

D. Shorten your swings if they are overpowering you and forcing you to miss.

E. Stay back and give yourself more time to execute.

They are aggressive; they rush the net.

A. Do not panic or try to overpower them. Hit the ball at their feet or over their heads.

B. Rush the net before they do to control the point.

C. Sunburn their eyeballs — lob a lot to frustrate them.

D. Take the pace off the ball to get at their feet or to bother them.

E. Both of you play on the baseline. Slow the game down.

They lob a lot.

A. Have patience. Keep the ball in play. Wait for the easy shot before you attempt a put-away.

B. Move back a few more feet off the net. You know a lob is coming.

C. Come to the net only behind strong shots. Hit your balls closer to their feet, so it is tougher for them to lob.

They hit a lot of balls at your feet.

A. Stop early enough to handle the shot.

B. Block the ball.

C. Only come in behind strong shots, so they can't hit your feet so easily.

D. Do not stay in no man's land. Hit your one shot and move in or back.

A fast ball comes at you.

A. Block — do not swing.

B. Probably lob back if you are near the baseline.

C. Get your shots at their feet, so they can't blast balls at you.

Opponents poach a lot.

A. Hit down their alley to keep them honest.

B. Lob. Go over their head if you cannot pass them.

C. Analyze why they are able to poach your shots. Are your returns traveling through the middle of the court?

They are putting a lot of balls away.

A. This is probably because you're giving them a high contact point. Keep your shots low to their feet.

B. If your balls are low and they put them away, they are just much better than you. Do not ever play them again, or sit back and lob everything to frustrate them.

Server's partner picks off a lot of returns.

A. Observe her to see if she plays navel tennis.

B. Mix up your returns. Are you predictable?

C. If her alley is open, try to hit it there to keep her honest.

D. Lob if you cannot hit the open court. The problem may be a strong serve.

They both play back.

A. Have patience. Wait for a ball close enough to the net, so you can angle a winner.

B. Hit short to pull them up. Do this only if their approach shots and volleys are weak.

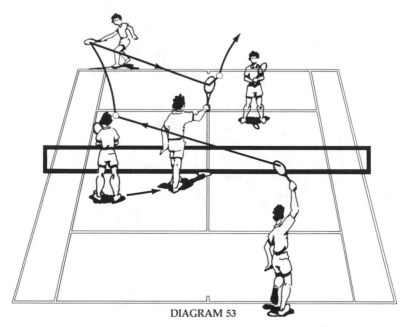

DIAGRAM 53

Here are two games, one as a receiving team and one as a serving team. You are the receiving team. (See accompanying Diagrams.)

Love-Love   Serve goes wide into service court. You return crosscourt. Server's partner is there waiting. He puts the ball away at the feet of your partner. Your return was fine. The server's partner should not have been there. (He should have been wide with the serve.) Give him this point. Next time burn his alley to keep him honest (Diagram 53).

15-Love   Receiver slugs return long. He does not get upset with his error. Next point, he will shorten his swing and hit more easily. He knows he should work into the match.

30-Love   Same wide serve. Server's partner moves again to the center. The alert receiver hits down the line for a winner (Diagram 54).

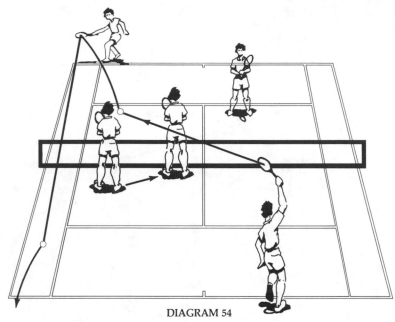

DIAGRAM 54

30-15   Receiver hits the return with control and
moves in. The server cannot control the
backhand shot and hits to receiver's
partner. Receiver's partner volleys ball
through center correctly. (See Diagram 55.)

30-30   Serve goes wide again. This time server's
partner stays. Receiver can now go
crosscourt and follow in his return. The
return is too short and to the server's
forehand. Server is able to hit ball at feet
of receiver. Receiver hits ball up to server's
partner. He correctly volleys ball through
center. Even though the receiving team lost
the point, they see a pattern in the
opponent's service placement. (See
Diagram 56.)

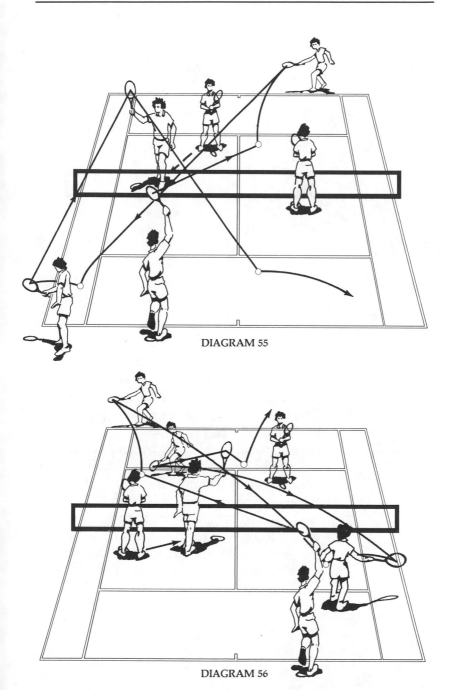

DIAGRAM 55

DIAGRAM 56

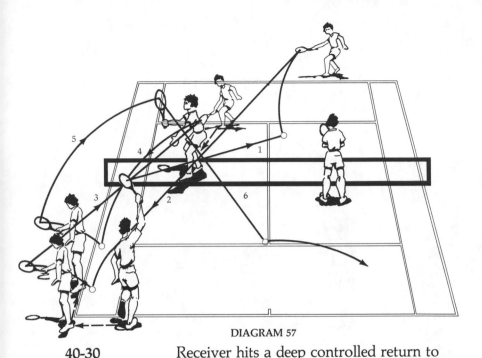

DIAGRAM 57

40-30

Receiver hits a deep controlled return to backhand of server again. Server again pops up the ball to the receiver's partner. Receiver's partner hasn't moved in this time, and the ball gets low to his feet. He cannot put the volley away and correctly hits the ball to the server's backhand again and moves in. He puts the next ball away. Receiver's partner will charge in tighter next time to ensure winning the point more easily. Receiving team realizes they gave the server a second chance, but the server cannot control his backhand. They have found a weakness. (See Diagram 57.)

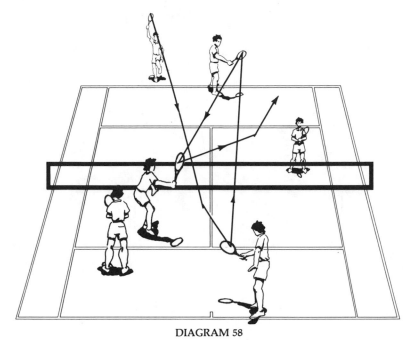

DIAGRAM 58

40-40   Strong serve to backhand. Server's partner
                   poaches and hits volley at receiver's
                   partner's feet. Receiving team realizes that
                   the serving team played a good point. Next
                   time the receiver may lob such a strong
                   serve and active net player.

Ad in   Server misses first serve. Receiver does not
                   move in for the second serve. Second serve
                   lands considerably shorter, and receiver
                   nets the return as he has to run in so far to
                   get it. He will catalog this and move in on
                   the second serve next time.

Game over.

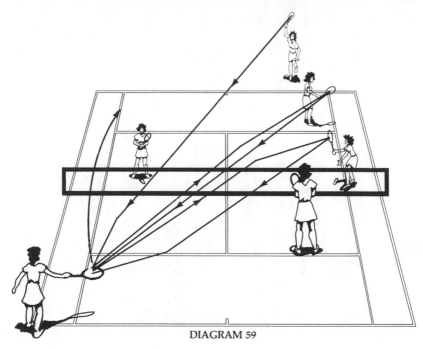

DIAGRAM 59

You are the serving team.

Love-Love   Excellent serve down the middle. Server's partner does not play navel tennis. She misses poaching opportunity. Receiver's partner does play navel tennis and picks off the server's return (Diagram 58).

Love-15   Return lands shallow. Receiver intelligently stays back. Server moves in to the net to hit the short ball. Server hits shot back to receiver. Receiver then hits high ball back to server. Server hits shot again back to receiver (close to deep). (She should have put the ball away through the net player.) Receiver takes advantage of another chance and hits a winning lob. (See Diagram 59.)

DIAGRAM 60

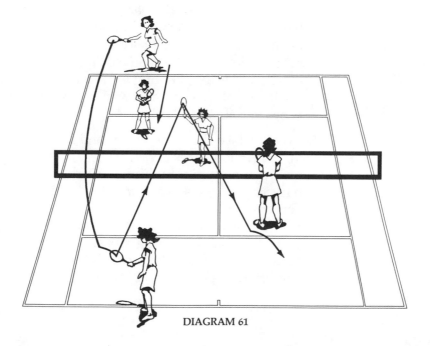

DIAGRAM 61

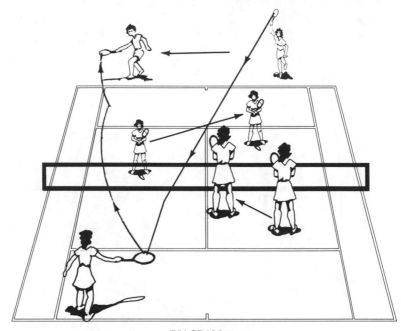

DIAGRAM 62

Love-30

Easy serve goes to receiver's forehand. She blasts return at server and moves in. Server realizes what a difficult shot is coming and blocks a lob over the receiver's partner — the closer person. Serving team moves into the lethal lob positon and wins point. (See Diagrams 60 and 61.)

15-30

Receiver lobs the serve return and moves in. Server lobs back short. Net player misses opportunity by hitting overhead back toward the server (close to deep). Server's partner has moved without the ball. She is now back on the baseline and saves the point by hitting a deep lob return. She rushes in afterwards for the winner. (See Diagrams 62 and 63.)

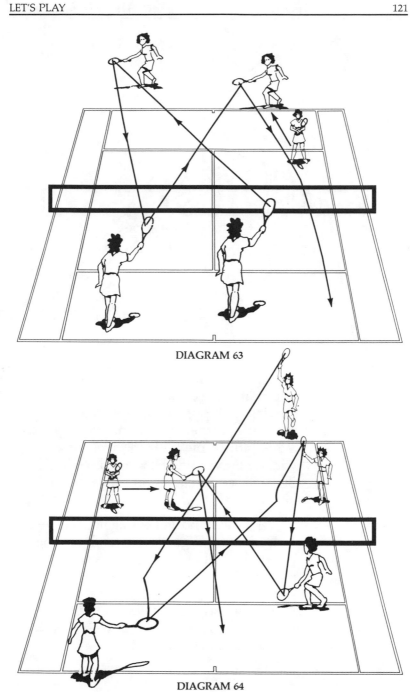

DIAGRAM 63

DIAGRAM 64

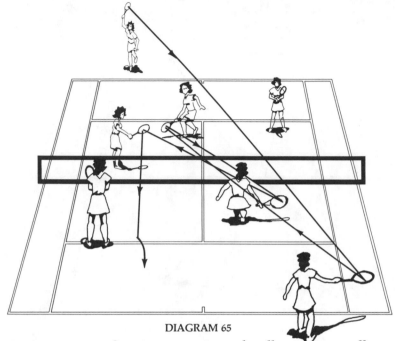

DIAGRAM 65

30-30   Server moves in and volleys. An excellent return at the feet catches the server still moving. She pops up an easy ball. An alert receiver's partner, moving in when she sees a low return, picks off the shot for a winner. Server will be more disciplined. She will set up earlier and stay set during her contact.

30-40   Server serves and volleys again. She gets a high return and goes close to close. She places the ball at the feet of receiver's partner. Receiver's partner makes a great save. Server's partner is shifting over — moving without the ball — and is in position to drive the ball at receiver's partner again (Diagram 64).

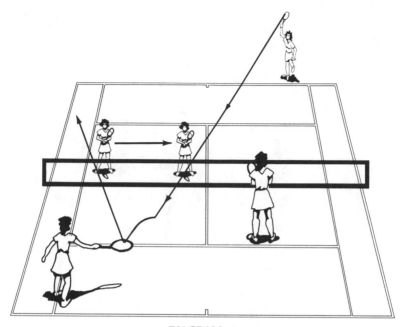

DIAGRAM 66

40-40   Server serves and volleys again. Receiver places excellent return to feet of server again. Server is stable and softly hits ball back to feet of oncoming receiver. Server closes net off to get the higher ball from the receiver. A perfectly played point for the serving team. The soft first volley was the key in winning the point. (See Diagram 65.)

Ad in   Easy second serve lands in center court. Server's partner mistakenly moves, eager to poach. But the second serve is too easy to handle, and receiver hits return down alley of server's partner for winner. (See Diagram 66.)

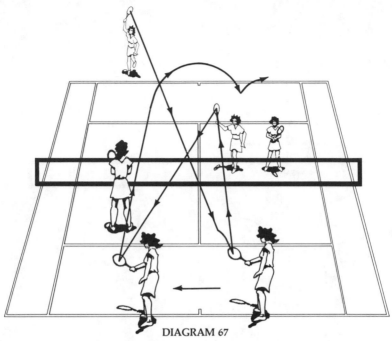

DIAGRAM 67

Deuce   Good serve down center. Server's partner poaches and hits shot down the center. Receiver moves without ball (Dial-A-Mate play) and saves point with a lob. Server is struggling after lob, so receiver's partner shifts into lethal lob play and picks off a floater back. (See Diagrams 67 and 68.)

Ad out   Server stays back. Receiver moves in after the return. Receiver gets next shot chest high on the service line (behind the most important line on the court). She tries to go from the center too wide (change flow) and unnecessarily misses volley (Diagram 69).

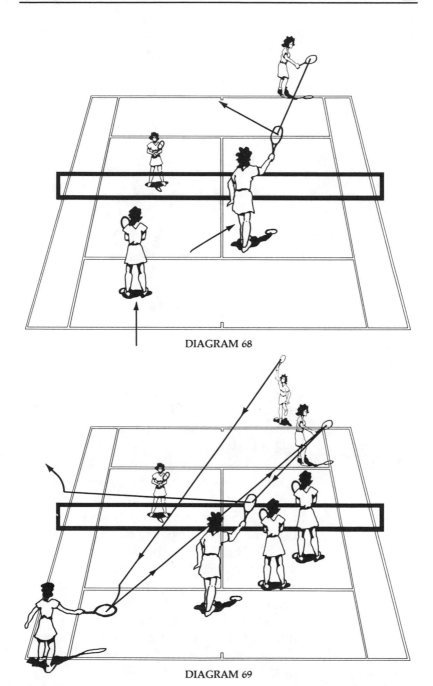

DIAGRAM 68

DIAGRAM 69

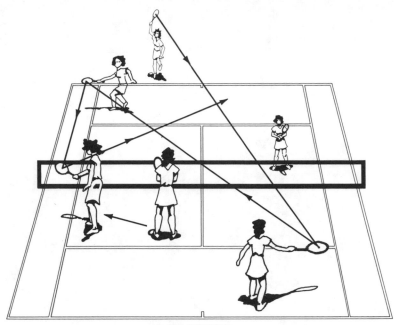

DIAGRAM 70

Duece

Server stays back. Server incorrectly reads the opponent's court position and tries to hit a passing shot down the line. Receiver's partner plays navel tennis and has the alley closed off. She puts the volley away. (See Diagram 70.)

Ad out

Receiver hits to server's partner. Server's partner volleys to receiver's partner waist high. This allows receiver's partner to get ball back. Server was standing and observing when her partner had an easy ball. She is not quick enough to move in and react to the next shot. The ball bounces twice before either player on the serving team can reach it. Server's partner should have gotten her volley lower to receiver's partner's feet. The server should have been moving forward when her partner had the set-up shot. (See Diagram 71.)

DIAGRAM 71

Game over.

Even though the team lost the first two games, they were learning. They gained awareness of the opponents' shot selection, court movement, and potential and limitations in their strokes. They were adjusting their shots to establish their consistency.

No one intentionally loses the first few games, but there is no reason to panic if you do. Establish your sense of rhythm, scout your opponents, and work into the match. Your game should be peaking at the end of the first set. Stay at this high level of performance throughout the second and, if needed, third set. Blasting a few winners early without a sense of "ball feel" will only lead to inconsistent play and frustration.

"Nirvana": mental toughness

You have read the previous pages and now understand the logic to the game of doubles. There are high-percentage and low-percentage shots; there are reasons to move to certain positions on the court; and there are reasons why you win and lose matches.

A major focus has been on the word *awareness*. A player has to be aware of many variables, recognize the different options, and choose the best one. At first it seems over-whelming and almost impossible to take it all in. But if you practice with a purpose and work at the On the Court drills, it eventually becomes clear and automatic. Perfect practice makes perfect play.

This book provides you with winning strategies. Ideally, this should be enough. Realistically, I know it is not. A clear head is needed to see all the variables. Players still panic, fear their opponents, concentrate poorly, and choke under pressure. For this reason I would like to say a few words about mental toughness.

This subject has enough material for a book in itself. A few authors have put some outstanding material together. Jim Loehr, a nationally recognized speaker and guru to top

professionals on the tour, has written a book entitled,
ATHLETIC EXCELLENCE: MENTAL TOUGHNESS
TRAINING FOR SPORTS. Mike Eikenberry of the Four
Star Tennis Academy and Bob Rotella of the University of
Virginia have put together an excellent cassette tape
program. If you wish to pursue this subject in depth, these
would be excellent sources.

Here are a few key ideas. The action happens so fast
during a point that there is no way you can think. You
have to rely on your instincts, your reflex actions. If your
reflex choices let you down, practice the drills more. If your
mind is cluttered with irrelevant or negative thoughts or if it
tends to wander, then practice a "mantra."

A mantra is a word or phrase repeated over and over
while meditating. This repetition focuses the mind to the
exclusion of all other thoughts. It is an aid to concentration.

In tennis, this repetitive thought should be centered on
the ball or the target. TENNIS IS A NON-COMPETITIVE
SPORT! As Jim Loehr says, the match is between you and
the ball and the target. Remove all other thoughts from
your mind during the point.

You may say the word "hit" as the ball hits your strings.
Another thought would be to say "yes" — sure beats going
"Oh, no!" The idea is to be so intent on saying these words
at contact that no distracting thoughts can interfere. Your
grooved stroke patterns and strategy training will instinc-
tively take over and produce the desired results.

If you panic or don't remember to aim for a target, you
may say "crosscourt" or "lob" as the ball is crossing the net
toward you.

If you have poor body discipline, you may use a
kinesthetic sense of body awareness and feel "head down"
or "back foot down" at contact.

The list could go on and on. Identify what mantra helps
you concentrate the best. Practice it each time you play, so
you can rely on it during a close match. You must learn to
get in good mental shape just as a person trains to get in
good physical shape.

Between points is when you have time to think. Analyze the flow of the match and the previous point. Always be ready and aware to make whatever adjustments are necessary. BE AWARE; DO NOT BE NEGATIVE OR CRITICAL! Negative feedback or self-recrimination between points only clutters the mind and tenses the body. Keep your mind free to be aware and highly sensitive to the variables. No match is static. Constant adjustments are always necessary.

Before you started reading this book, you had your grooved stroke patterns. This book has given you a systematic way to understand strategy and tactics used in doubles. If you have mastered both of these, then trust yourself. Stop dwelling on them during a point and shift your attention to a mantra that will aid you in achieving excellent concentration and an uncluttered mind. If you can do this, you will obviously be playing at your best every time you step on the court. This is why you should be playing — for the self-satisfaction, the thrill of achieving. All well-adjusted persons and mature competitors know the lessons learned along the way are as valuable, if not more valuable, than the skill attained. Do not feel bad about mistakes. Do not apologize for being human. Continually strive for excellence.

Best of luck! Enjoy your doubles!

On the court
1. Think of several words or thoughts to focus on during the point.
2. Play several points. Practice these different mantras. Understand which ones distract you and which ones help your concentration.
3. Play several games. Repeat your mantra during each hit of every point. Try to work at closing off all other thoughts.
4. Play points. Between points analyze what is happening. What needs to be done to sustain the winning? What needs to be changed to stop the losing?

5. Play points. Switch sides after odd games and analyze the match — ten to sixty seconds — with your partner. Stop at the net post with your partner. Put your racquet down. (Take a mental break.) Towel off, take a sip of water, and walk to the other side refreshed and ready.

Positive self-talk

1. I have identified my mantra.
2. I am getting better and better at my concentration abilities.
3. I am able to repeat my mantra during points. I do not panic under pressure.
4. I am getting better at analyzing the match between points. I understand my opponents' tactics.
5. I know when to change a losing game.
6. I stay relaxed and confident when playing important points.

Mixed troubles and other questions

HOW DO YOU PLAY MIXED DOUBLES?

Mixed doubles is played either socially or competitively. Without this clear distinction, we have mixed-up doubles or worse yet — mixed troubles.

Play competitive mixed doubles like any other match. Hit the high-percentage shot. Play the weaker player.

But most mixed doubles are social in nature. Guys should lighten up and get rid of any male ego problems. The friendship of the couple with whom you are playing and respect for one's spouse should be more important than winning a tennis match.

Men should not smash balls at the opposing woman in social mixed doubles. They should put the ball away by placing it at her feet or angle the ball by her. Husbands should let their wives have some fun and not criticize them constantly. Instead, they should be congratulated for taking up the sport.

Of course, everything applies equally for the wife if she is a better player than her husband. Whichever the case, enjoy the camaraderie and exercise; fight the ego battles somewhere else.

How do you choose a partner? There are four factors to consider.

1. Are you compatible? It is important that you have a good working relationship on the court. You must have a partner that you can talk to easily, even after you have missed a set-up to give your opponents the first set. How well you get along off the court is often an indication of how well you will get along on the court.

2. Are you complementary? Every good doubles team has one player who is very steady and one who can put the ball away. Ideally, each player can perform both tasks. However, if both players are steady but are afraid to finish off the point, then there is not enough pressure put on the opponents. If both players go for the winners and commit a lot of unforced errors, then they make it too easy for the opponents. Be aware of how your styles of play match up.

3. Are you at the same level? You should be of relatively equal abilities. A noticeably weaker player will be picked on during a match, and the weaker player may therefore feel inadequate. The stronger player may also resent the inability of the partner to win more points. Finding a player of similar skill simplifies things.

4. Do you have the same motivation and goals? If you wish to drill four times a week, and your partner wants to play four times a year, you are going to have problems. The harder-working player feels the less active partner is not doing his or her share. The person who plays more will probably be a much better player in a short time.

Keep these thoughts in mind, and you should have plenty of great doubles matches.

Who receives from which side? The answer is whichever way works better. Here are some guidelines.

1. The deuce court is the more difficult court from which to receive. It is awkward to hit a backhand return — assuming you are right-handed.

2. The deuce court receiver will hit the first return point

and more returns throughout the match. You may place the steadier player here. You can then aim at getting a good start each game.

3. The ad court player has the pressure points — ad in, ad out. The player who rises to the occasion may play this side.

4. With one right-handed and one left-handed player, you usually have the forehands in the center, because most balls will be hit down the center.

How do I warm up? Players miss a great opportunity by abusing and misunderstanding the warm-up.

The warm-up period is used to scout your opponents and create your own sense of rhythm and confidence. The warm-up is not used to blast errors or practice making bad calls!

The following can serve as a model. Allow yourself plenty of time to drive to the match. Place yourself in the proper frame of mind before you leave the house. If you are too excited, calm yourself. If you are apathetic, psyche yourself up. Rehearse the match as you are driving the car. See yourself winning points. See yourself executing properly, choosing the proper targets. See yourself winning the match.

Arrive at the match site fifteen minutes to one-half hour prior to your starting time. Find a quiet place. Do some light jogging and practice shadow strokes. Now do your stretching. Remember to stretch easily. Pain is not gain. Focus on what you are going to do correctly during the match throughout this time.

You are now ready for the pre-match warm-up. HIT SLOW, SOFT BALLS AT FIRST! The warm-up should be used to gain a feel for the court surface, the speed of your opponent's shots, etc. By hitting balls slowly it is easier to get used to the conditions. Control all your shots to one spot in front of your opponent. Do not think you are hitting balls to your opponent. You are aiming the ball to a spot or target on the court. IF YOU CAN'T HIT ONE SPOT IN A WARM-UP, YOU CAN'T HIT ALL SPOTS IN

A MATCH! Hit the ball at the speed you can totally control; then gradually raise the speed to your maximum level.

As you are gaining your sense of feel, simultaneously warm up your body. Start at the head and work your way down.

Warm up your eyes. Start focusing on the ball. Get your mind and your eyes to follow the ball all the way into your racquet. See it leave your opponent's racquet and come back. Next warm up your arms. As mentioned above, start off stroking easily and gradually build. By the time all this is done, you should be loose. Now start moving your feet a lot. Get that footwork going!

Scouting your opponent should also occur during the warm up. Be tacky: critically examine your opponent. Is she heavy? Will she be slow? Does she have a bad backhand? Can you capitalize on it? Did she trip over the baseline walking onto the court? Is she uncoordinated? Does she not take any overheads? Maybe she hates that shot. Look at your opponent, her strokes, her consistency. Make some hard judgments that may be useful during the match. Identify the weaker opponent — the one you will aim most of your shots toward during the match.

Does she warm up intelligently? If she is erratic, it will be difficult for you to establish your sense of rhythm and timing. You will have to do this in the first few games. Work into the match. It is frustrating to warm up against someone like this. The silver lining is that she should be just as erratic during the match.

How do I handle easy second serves? This is a tempting shot to smash back at the server. If your timing is great — go ahead. However, this is a drastic change of flow — slow serve to a fast return. You can defeat your opponents by staying in the flow. Shorten the swing on your return and block the easy serve sharply crosscourt. Your shot will land near the service line and singles sideline. This will pull the server out of the court as well as make her run several steps. Your partner can move in for the kill.

Summary

It is evident that good doubles involves a high level of cooperation and teamwork. A player must know what her partner will be hitting. This allows her to move without the ball — shift into position before the opponent makes contact with her shot.

General laws to follow:
1. Hit deep to deep, close to close. Your partner will always know which opponent will be hitting the next shot.
2. Go with the flow. Your partner will know where you will be aiming your next shot, and what type of shot it will be. She can anticipate and is free to move earlier.
3. Aim at the feet. Do not hit beyond your control level. Your partner will be more confident at the net and have more freedom to poach.
4. Do not self destruct. Go for set-up shots until you have all three variables in your favor. Do not make errors behind the "most important line on the court." Strive to get the first ball in.
5. Be center conscious. Aim the majority of shots toward the center. This allows you to leave alleys unguarded and limits the options of your opponents.

Good doubles demands discipline:
1. Get balanced on your shots.
2. Get set on your volleys when attacking the net.
3. Observe the "Rhythm Method of Ball Control."
4. Have disciplined shot selection. Choose high-percentage shots.
5. Have patience. Keep your emotions under control. Do not panic. The only crucial point to win in the match is the last one.

Doubles demands a high level of awareness:
1. Observe your opponents. Notice their contact point, court position, and body position.
2. Know your contact point, court position, and body position.
3. Know your potential and limitations. Choose the correct shot.
4. Read the level of your opponents' skill. Anticipate their next shot.
5. Critique the flow of the match between points. Change a losing strategy. Hold firm to a winning strategy.
6. Be aware of your number of unforced errors.
7. Be aware of what contact point you are giving your opponents.